c.s.lewis **The story teller**

c.s.lewis

The story teller

by derick
bingham

For
Douglas Gresham
who has so faithfully
guarded the flame of
C. S. Lewis,

for Ross Wilson
who has so skilfully
sculpted it
and

for Keith Getty
who has so movingly set it
to music.

Important Note:

This is a true story. All the events actually took place.
The more important conversations are based on what
people really did say at the time. The less important
conversations, and some background details, are
imagined.

©1999 Derick Bingham
ISBN 1-85792-487-8

Published by Christian Focus Publications Ltd
Geanies House, Fearn ,Tain, Ross-shire, IV20 1TW,
Scotland, Great Britain.

Cover Illustration by Mark Vinney

Printed and Bound in Great Britain by Caledonian

Introduction

It was late afternoon and I was driving in heavy traffic on the Malone Road in Belfast, Northern Ireland.

Suddenly I noticed a friend of mine driving his Saab in the traffic.

"It's Ross!" I thought, and with hand gestures I asked him to follow me. He waved back his agreement.

"Good to see you, Derick," he said as he got out of his car in my driveway, "I have something to show you."

I love surprises and fascinated I watched as Ross, on entering my home, took off the plastic cover of a model for a bronze sculpture he was making to erect in our city.

It was a model of a man with a book in his hand, heading for a wardrobe.

"It's from the story, *The Lion, The Witch and The Wardrobe*, Christopher," I explained to a little four year old boy who was in my home that afternoon.

"The man is C. S. Lewis who wrote the story".

"Where does the wardrobe lead to, Christopher?" asked my wife.

"Narnia", answered Christopher, "Where the White Witch lives and it is always winter."

Millions of children around the world have in their imagination been through that wardrobe and into the land of Talking Beasts.

Aslan is loving but never tame and he does not hesitate to bowl children over or put a scratch on them to turn them away from worse danger ahead.

The White Witch, of course, kills Aslan but he comes to life again. There is something about the Lion, though. He is mysterious, tough but incredibly kind.

Once, a little ten year old girl called Ann Jenkins wrote to Professor C. S. Lewis with a question she had about something he had written. She was delighted to receive a reply.

Historically, it is one of C. S. Lewis' most important letters because it is telling a little girl, in simple language, what he was driving at in his writing of the seven Chronicles of Narnia, Chronicles that millions of children now read all over the world.

Here is what he said in his letter...

Magdalen College,
Cambridge

5th March 1961

Dear Ann,

What Aslan meant when he said he had died is, in one sense plain enough. Read the earlier book in this series called, "The Lion, The Witch and The Wardrobe" and you will find the full story of how he was killed by the White Witch and came to life again. When you have read that, I think you will probably see that there is a deeper meaning behind it. The whole Narnian story is about Christ. That is to say, I ask myself, "Supposing there really was a world like Narnia and supposing it had (like our world) gone wrong and supposing Christ wanted to go into that world and save it (as He did ours) what might have happened?" The stories are my answer.

Since Narnia is a world of Talking Beasts, I thought He would become a Talking Beast there as He became a man here. I pictured Him becoming a lion there because (a) the lion is supposed to be the king of beasts: (b) Christ is called the "Lion of Judah" in the Bible: (c) I had been having strange dreams about lions when I began the work. The whole series works out like this:

"The Magician's Nephew" tells the Creation and how evil entered Narnia.

"The Lion, The Witch and The Wardrobe" tells the Crucifixion and Resurrection.

"Prince Caspian" tells the Restoration of the true religion after a corruption.

"The Horse and His Boy" tells the calling and conversion of a heathen.

"The Voyage of the Dawn Treader" tells of spiritual life (especially in Reepicheep).

"The Silver Chair" tells of the continued war against the powers of darkness.

"The Last Battle" tells of the coming of the Anti-Christ (The Ape) the end of the world and the last judgment.

All clear?
Yours,

C. S. Lewis.

*See page 178

If you ever come to Belfast you can see my friend Ross Wilson's statue at the Holywood Arches with C. S. Lewis' letter to Ann Jenkins in bronze on the back of the wardrobe. You could also travel further through East Belfast until you arrive at the Circular Road where there still stands a beautiful house called, "Little Lea". If you had been there at the beginning of the century you would have found two little boys playing in an attic up in the roof in quite a fascinating little kingdom of their own. There were little passages through which they could crawl, and secret hiding places like the cistern room which became the model for the beginning of the Narnia adventures in *The Magician's Nephew*. For, of course, one of those little boys was Clive Staples Lewis. Let me tell you the fascinating story of his life.

Derick Bingham

Written in the Centenary year
of C. S. Lewis - 1998

Contents Page

'I bagsy this attic
as my study,'
said Clive,
'I will write my stories here.'

Tarantulas, Ghosts and Stories

Some of the most beautiful sunsets in the island of Ireland are to be found touching the Antrim Hills and the shores of Belfast Lough. The house called 'Little Lea' is often touched by the rays of the sinking sun and when C. S. Lewis moved to live there as a boy of seven, open fields lay to the front of the house and ran down to the shores of the Lough.

"I bagsy this attic as my study," said Clive exploring an attic in the roof, "I will write my stories here."

"Stories?" you might ask. C.S. Lewis loved stories. Throughout his life he found it really hard to make anything by hand. He had only one joint in his thumb and therefore couldn't make anything with scissors and cardboard. He longed to make ships and houses and engines from card and paper and stuff but it only ended in tears. He could, though, hold a pencil or a pen and was driven to write stories instead. It was a blessing in disguise!

Many years later C. S. Lewis wrote that you can do more with a castle in a story than with the best cardboard castle that ever stood on a nursery table. Millions of children were to be very glad that he loved that attic at 'Little Lea' for it became the model for the beginning of the adventures into Narnia.

On wet, windy, afternoons as well as on sunlit days the two small boys escaped into a fantasy land; the world they invented was called Boxen. It was a land that animals inhabited as humans inhabit ours. Clive wrote stories of brave mice and rabbits who rode out dressed as armour clad knights - to kill cats.

"Warren, you can add the trains and steamships as we plot Animal Land together," said Clive to his brother.

The fact was that Warren and Clive hardly ever had a pencil or pen out of their hand. Warren loved drawing steamships and trains and Clive delighted in drawing dressed animals. They drew maps of Animal Land, Warren, of course, mapping the main shipping routes from Animal Land, and the special island they created. It was called India like the country in the real world but this India was a world of their own creation.

Every summer the Lewis family went off to the seaside for a holiday. The boys loved it, and their mother, Flora did too. She was an attractive, university graduate and a highly intelligent woman. She even taught her boys French and Latin.

"To be quite honest I find holidays by the sea very tedious," their father Albert would tell his friends. He was a busy solicitor, a handsome looking man with a moustache and he could be found, on summer holidays, wandering up and down the beach constantly looking at his watch and obviously longing to be back at work.

"What on earth are you saying, Clive?" Flora asked her little boy on one of their summer holidays.

"He is Jacksie!" answered Clive, pointing to himself.

"Jacksie?" said Flora with exasperation.

"He is Jacksie!" insisted Clive. What was Clive talking about? He was in fact wanting himself to be called after a little dog who had lived near his home and who had sadly got run over.

Amazingly from that moment on Clive refused to be called by any other name but Jack. For the rest of his life C. S. Lewis became known as "Jack's" to his family and Jack to his friends, so, from now on in this book we will call him Jack too.

"Calm down, Jack, please calm down," said Flora holding her son close after he woke one night in a cold sweat from some dreams he was having.

"Why do I have these terrifying dreams, mother?" Jack asked.

"What do you see in your dreams, Jack?"

"Huge tarantula spiders!" answered her

frightened son. "And lots of ghosts."

Jack suffered from a very vivid imagination and that very imagination was eventually to turn him into one of the greatest storytellers of the twentieth century. Fortunately his imagination was not always filled with tarantulas and ghosts.

One day Warren rushed into Jack's room. "Have a look at this!" he said, excitedly. In his hand Warren had a biscuit tin lid on which he had created a miniature toy garden with twigs and flowers, covered with moss. It fired Jack's imagination in a very deep way and he called it "The first beauty I ever saw." For the rest of his life Jack imagined Paradise to have something of Warren's toy garden.

"Was there ever a house like this house for books?" thought Annie Harper, Jack and Warren's Governess, who was an excellent teacher. She was right. There were books in the study, books in the drawing room, books in the cloakroom, books, two deep on the bookcase, in the bookcase in the landing, books in a bedroom, books piled high in the attic. Books, books and more books were all over the house for Albert never got rid of any of the books he bought.

Jack was allowed to read any book he liked, and he read them constantly. From the writing of Conan Doyle to Mark Twain, from E. Nesbit and her book *The Phoenix and The Wishing Carpet* to *Gulliver's Travels*, from

Beatrix Potter to Longfellow's poetry, Jack was touched by the power of words. He lived in his imagination.

"You are such a little chatterbox," said Lizzie Endicott, the boys' nurse. Lizzie was from County Down and in her the boys saw no flaw. All his life C. S. Lewis could never be called a snob. He never looked down upon people, whatever their background. Less than a mile from his home stood a huge house called "Mountbracken" where some titled relatives lived and he visited often. He never forgot that good people can be found in all sorts of places in life. He knew how to relate to ordinary people as well as intelligent, university types.

Sadly, though, Jack's snug and peaceful life in 'Little Lea', the house of long corridors, sunlit roofs and fascinating attics was shattered by a great loss.

One night he was feeling quite ill and started to cry. His head ached and his tooth throbbed. The pathetic whimpers from the little boys room would have broken your heart.

"Why does my mother not come to me?" he kept crying out as he tossed and turned in bed. "Please get her to come."

But his mother didn't come. There were noises coming and going all over 'Little Lea'. Doors opened and doors shut. There were anxious murmurings of one kind and another and then, at last, his father came. He was crying.

21

"Jack," he said, tenderly, "your mother has cancer. There will have to be an operation here in our house. Hopefully it will lead to a cure."

But it didn't. Gradually Flora Lewis was overcome by the disease and her two small boys were kept at a distance from her delirium and pain.

"Warnie," said Jack to his brother, "we need each other more than ever before."

"I'm here Jack," said Warren. "You need not be afraid." The two young brothers grew closer and closer.

"Father's temper is frightening," said Jack, as he witnessed his poor father come under the huge pressure of anxiety for his dying wife. Albert Lewis could do nothing to help his wife. Under extreme stress he would say wild things.

Jack prayed to God that his mother would recover. He was sure there would be a miracle. His whole idea of God through his childhood was that God was some kind of magician. He did not know him as Saviour nor as Judge. He had neither fear nor awe nor love for Him and he expected that when He had answered his prayer He would simply go away. But God did not cure Flora Lewis and He also did not go away. Jack was, one day, to come to know Him through Jesus Christ and his whole attitude to God was to change. That day, though, was still a long way off.

Flora Lewis died in 1908 and all Jack's pain at her death was to surface later in the character of Digory in *The Magician's Nephew*. And there was a lot of pain.

Security vanished from Jack's life when his mother died. She had been an anchor for him, someone to turn to. In her presence he had felt tranquillity and happiness. Later on he reported that "There was to be much fun, many pleasures, many stabs of joy; but no more of the old security. It was all sea and islands now; the great continent had sunk like Atlantis".

" Joy, was not only absent
but forgotten. "

C.S. Lewis
on his school days at Wynard

'Oldie' Rules! Not O.K.

The Fleetwood boat slowly moved away from the quay at Belfast. On the deck, waving goodbye to their father, were Jack and Warren Lewis. Jack was on his way to school for the first time. He was about to become what is known as a "boarder".

"Goodbye Dad, take care," they shouted.

"Goodbye lads and keep your chins up," replied Albert Lewis standing sadly in the damp twilight of that September evening in 1908. Poor Jack, he didn't know the misery that was about to envelop his life.

"Come on Jack! I'll show you round the ship," said Warren who had been drawing ships for almost as long as Jack could remember. Eagerly Jack followed looking into every corner of the night ferry as she slipped down Belfast Lough with the lights of Ireland receding.

"I hate these new school clothes, Warnie," said Jack, pulling at his thick, prickly suit made of heavy serge material, "As for these knicker-bockers, they are buttoned so tightly below my knee they have left a red mark on my leg!"

"Ah Jack, that high and stiff Eton collar may be worn by all public schoolboys but was never made for you!" said Warnie. "Even these stiff new boots of mine make my feet ache!" said Jack.

"These horrid hard bowler hats are just ridiculous, Jack," said Warren, "but school rules are school rules."

Soon the boys were in their bunks and when the wind got up in the night the ship began to roll.

Jack proved to be a better sailor than the heavily sea-sick Warren. They were both glad to disembark around six o'clock in the morning.

After boarding the train at the station they were soon heading south across an England that Jack, amazingly, first found extremely disappointing. As the steam engine pulled them from Fleetwood to Euston the more Jack saw of the country the more he disliked it.

"It's so flat, Warnie," said Jack. "No sea. No stone hedges. No white cottages."

"The fields are much bigger here, Jack," answered Warnie, "but the haystacks are the wrong shape!" Jack was missing the hills of County Down already. His dislike of England was to last for quite some time.

If Jack first disliked England, he was to actually detest his new school at Wynard in Watford even more. It was a small preparatory school with nine boarders and around nine day boys. It was run by a frighteningly extraordinary man whom the boys nicknamed 'Oldie'.

"Oh! There you are Rees, you horrid boy,"
'Oldie' might say on entering the classroom after
breakfast, "If I'm not too tired I shall give you a
good drubbing this afternoon." He gave most of
his pupils a good drubbing. He would even, at
times, make a boy bend down at one end of the
classroom and then take a run across the room's
length for each stroke he would give him. One boy
to whom he gave dozens of thrashings resolved
never to make a sound. He never did until the end
of the thrashing when a strange rattling cry would
come from him as the rest of the school-boys
watched in deathly silence.

'Oldie', it would seem, was actually insane
and was even known to leap up and dance around
the classroom like a performing bear.

There was a lot of arithmetic done at Wynard
School and precious little else. At the end of each
morning 'Oldie' would shout at each pupil, "How
many sums have you done, boy?"

"Five," Warren would answer.

"But you always say five, Warren, every
morning," said Jack to his brother.

"I do indeed, Jack, and I tell the truth but the
fact is I do the same five sums every day!"

The teaching staff consisted of only three
people, the Headmaster, nicknamed 'Oldie', his
grown-up son, nicknamed 'Wee Wee', and an
usher. The ushers by and large didn't last very
long. One, in fact, only lasted for a week! As

supervision was extremely slack and very little assistance was given to the boys in doing their endless arithmetic, Jack's brother had discovered that he could get away with doing the same five sums every day.

The food at Wynard was simply awful. The beds were freezing cold. The toilets were stinking. Life was thoroughly miserable. "Joy," C. S. Lewis wrote later, "was not only absent but forgotten." He later nicknamed the school Belsen, after the German Concentration Camp where dreadful atrocities had happened during the Second World War.

On half-holidays, though, Jack and his friends were allowed to go for walks. They bought sweets in village shops, pottered about along the canal and sat on grassy banks watching for trains coming out of railway cuttings. The life of all the boys, though, was united by a hatred and fear of 'Oldie'.

At night Jack lay in the great curtainless dormitory at Wynard, gazing out at the night sky as other boys slept. He gazed at the moon and the stars and listened to the wind. At times there were thunderstorms and quite often he saw fog swirling around the school. It all became a world full of mystery and magic to him. Later he was to very skilfully reproduce his memories in creating night scenes in his Narnia stories. Reading these scenes in his books you can picture the heart of winter in Narnia and even feel the freezing cold of the frost and snow.

The Story-teller

The cold remote light of the moon often touched everything Jack saw from his dormitory hide out. The moon seemed to turn everything into an enchanted world in his imagination. It is interesting that many of the adventures that C. S. Lewis later wrote about took place by moonlight. Different children who arise in his books all dislike school and often find wonderful adventures at night-time. Take, for example, Jill Pole in her book, *The Silver Chair*. Jill, commissioned by the Great Lion Aslan to find the lost Prince Rilian had to fly through the night on the back of a great owl. Lewis wrote about Jill's experiences as she magically flew through the night on the back of the owl that mysteriously lands on her window sill.

"Though the sky was overcast one patch of watery silver showed where the moon was hiding above the clouds ... There was a certain amount of wind - a hustling, rustling sort of wind which meant that rain was coming soon."

This is just the sort of scene Jack would have gazed at from the dormitory window - many years before he wrote *The Silver Chair*.

To be able to go home to Ireland on school holidays after a cruel and seemingly endless term was, for Jack, like a release from prison. The joy of being at home at 'Little Lea' was a joy that was deeply felt. Fortunately, as well as inevitably, the Wynard school folded in 1910. Albert Lewis had to look for a new school for Jack. To be fair, Albert had no idea what a mess he had made of his first choice. Now he decided to send Jack to board at the large red-bricked Campbell College in Belfast about a mile from his home. Jack could come home on Sundays.

It was a school founded in order to give Ulster boys a public school education without them having to cross over the Irish Sea. It was a busy school with so much coming and going that Jack described it as like living permanently in a large railway station! Jack was twelve years of age when he went to Campbell College and unfortunately there were many fights on which the boys would take bets and a lot of yelling and shouting from the inevitable crowds of spectators who would look on. There was also quite a lot of bullying.

"Grab him!" said the crowd of boys, taking Jack by the arms and dragging him along a lot of corridors. He was taken to a half dark room where several other boys had been "captured".

"Bend down," they said to each of their captives and then, as if by magic, each captive disappeared after a shove.

"Now you," they said to Jack, and suddenly he found himself falling through a hole in a wall into what was the coal cellar. Locked in he heard his captors whooping with pleasure at how many captives they had bagged! Soon a very dirty and cramped Jack Lewis was let out.

It was all very mild in comparison to 'Oldie's Belsen'. Jack, in fact, did not suffer very much from bullying. He had an excellent English Literature teacher nicknamed 'Octie' who introduced him to a love of poetry which never left him. 'Octie' had no idea that the twelve year old boy sitting in his English class would one day become the best selling Christian author of all time. Three dozen of C.S. Lewis' titles would still be available with over forty million in print at the end of the century. An incredible number of people would come to faith in Jesus Christ through C. S. Lewis' writing. This, though, was a long way off. Meanwhile, Jack had his mind opened to the beauty and power of poetry as the leaves swirled down from the trees on to the Campbell College green in that autumn term of 1910.

'Octie' had a real name which was J. A. McNeill and his influence upon the boy who sat before him was greater than he ever knew.

Half way through his first term at Campbell College Jack took ill and his father, who for some reason was unhappy about the College, brought Jack home for six weeks. They were to be among the happiest six weeks of his life. He and his father drew very close. He read and wrote and drew to his hearts content. His father was out all day. 'Little Lea' with its large empty and silent rooms were described by Jack as being like "A refreshing bath after the crowded noise of Campbell".

As Christmas 1910 began to appear all over Belfast with its twinkling lights and mysterious presents under thousands of Christmas trees, it proved to be a snug and enjoyable time for the Lewis family at 'Little Lea'.

Little did the family know of the coming war clouds in Europe and that soon on an average day on the Western Front 2,533 men were to be killed in action, 9,121 were to be wounded and 1,164 were to go missing. The British Army would live in candlelit dug-outs and trenches hewn from Fricourt chalk or La Basse clay.

"Life, is only
term, holidays,
term, holidays,
till we leave school,
and then
work, work, work,
till we die!"

C.S. Lewis aged thirteen.

Life with Tubbs

"Hand me another cigarette Warnie," said the thirteen year old Jack. The pair of them felt very sophisticated as they sat in the Lime Street Hotel in Liverpool lolling in comfortable chairs reading magazines as they waited to catch the afternoon train south to school. The long boat journey from Belfast was over and they just loved the morning freedom.

The train arrived, at last. Jack found himself eventually entering the tall, white school building with a headmaster as different from 'Oldie' as day is from night. Here he was to be, for a change, well cared for.

"Welcome to Cherbourg, Jack," said the cheerful Matron on Jack's arrival with twenty other boarders, "I trust you will be very happy here".

As it turned out, he was, particularly because the Matron was so helpful to the boys. Kind, considerate, she comforted them. These boys were far from their parents so it was Matron who nursed them when they were sick and encouraged them in their work and school life when they were well. Jack, who had so recently lost his mother, was very fond of the Matron.

Sadly, though, and unintentionally, the Matron did huge damage to Jack's belief in the basic truths of Christianity. She talked to the boys on all kinds of subjects and always treated them as intelligent people. She was not a Christian but was desperately seeking for a settled faith. She had become deeply influenced by the occult and the whole idea of getting in touch with the spirit world. As she spoke of her interest in spiritualism Jack was suddenly gripped by the whole idea.

"Little by little," he wrote, "she ... blunted all the sharp edges of my belief... I was soon altering 'I believe' to 'one does feel' ... there was nothing to be obeyed and nothing to be believed except what was either comforting or exciting."

Jack was influenced to think along the lines that he needn't believe anything that was uncomfortable or that he found uninteresting. He would believe in what was 'comforting' or 'exciting'. But Jack recognised in later years that it was not just the Matron who was responsible for his unbelief. He recognised that the evil one, or the devil had influenced him and led him down the wrong path. In the end it was the devil and Jack's own sinful nature that made him listen to the Matron and her mistaken, sinful view of life.

Although Jack flourished intellectually under the leadership of the Headmaster of Cherbourg, nicknamed 'Tubbs', he began to have a depressing and negative attitude to the world in general. His studies in Latin and English flourished under 'Tubbs' and he was looked on as a very promising candidate for a scholarship to Malvern College. A gloom, though, seemed to be cast over him.

"Life," said Jack to a friend one day, "Is only term, holidays, term, holidays, till we leave school, and then work, work, work, till we die!"

It is amazing, in life, how one incident can deeply affect a person and their whole attitude to life. He began to have a very deep hatred towards a certain teacher at Cherbourg because that teacher had forbidden him to give anything to a beggar who came regularly to the school gates.

Jack, who was quite a tender hearted boy, could not understand why he was not allowed to show kindness to the beggar. Slowly, be began to be disillusioned with people and their lack of kindness to each other. He became extremely pessimistic about life saying that "everything would do what you did not want it to do".

Whatever you wanted to remain straight, would bend; whatever you tried to bend would fly back to the straight; all knots which you wished to be firm would come untied; all knots you wanted to untie would remain firm." He found words that summed up his rising atheism. They were words by Lucretius:

"Had God designed the world, it would not be
A world so frail and faulty as we see."

Half way through Jack's time at Cherbourg school, which lasted from 1911 to 1913, he came very heavily under the influence of a teacher whom Jack nicknamed 'Pogo'. A real man-about-town, 'Pogo' was clever and humorous. He taught the boys to pay a lot of attention to the clothes they wore, to feel like men of the world.

Jack records that under the influence of this man he began to become snobbish. He plastered his hair with oil and learned all the latest jokes; and 'Pogo' was clearly willing to explain in the jokes what Jack did not understand, whether good or bad. Jack also gave in to sexual temptation. He began to have, he noted, "the desire for glitter, swagger, distinction, the desire to be in the know". Jack looked back with sadness on this part of his life. He regretted how 'Pogo' had destroyed 'the child-like' and 'self-forgetful qualities' that he had possessed up to that point. Jack's ambitions now lay elsewhere. He wanted nothing more than to be "a fop, a cad, and a snob".

He also began to feel deep sexual lust for his dancing mistress. The truth was, Jack was growing up and sadly did not have the balance of Christian faith to overcome what the Bible calls, "The fiery darts of the evil one". He had lost faith in a loving Heavenly Father whose hand was behind the universe waiting to bring him joy. He found even the vastness of space menacing and unfriendly.

"Let's go to the Empire, Jack," said Warren on arrival in Liverpool at the end of term and having some time to wait before getting the boat for Belfast.

Invariably, the boys had their supper at a restaurant, usually poached eggs and tea, and Warren was always keen to go to the Empire Theatre where there was variety entertainment of songs and comic turns.

"I am not so sure I like those shows Warnie," said Jack, "I hate it when the acts go wrong and the comics don't get the laughs they were expecting." His father, though, loved to go out on a Saturday night in Belfast to the Belfast Hippodrome. When it was the boys' holidays they would often go out together. Jack though enjoying being out for a night looked forward much more to the incredibly delicious pies prepared by their domestic cook, Annie Strachan. Anybody who has ever had a taste of Irish cooking will know why Jack looked forward to his supper!

Towards the end of Jack's time at Cherbourg School he picked up a literary magazine one day and gazed at a headline and a picture. The title of the book was *Siegfreid and the Twilight of the Gods*. He said for him at that moment the sky "turned round". Although Jack knew nothing of the book, he saw a very powerful illustration in it of this old Norse saga. The illustration had been drawn delicately and powerfully by an artist called Arthur Rackham. Suddenly there stirred in him a deep sense of "pure Northernness". It was a feeling for vast distances, wild and remote lands. It was a vision of huge cold empty spaces that lay beyond the Atlantic and of the long, cool twilight of Northern summers for even in the Shetland Islands you could read a newspaper at Mid-night in your summer garden! He felt as if a voice was calling him from far away and he had visions of beauty that lay beyond the immediate. He became fascinated by Richard Wagner's music, particularly where he immortalised the Norse Legends in which Siegfreid is a great hero. In the last century Wagner composed four musical dramas around these legends. Jack bought records containing four operas of Wagner. These fired his imagination tremendously. He wrote a long poem about the story of Siegfreid which went into four books.

One summer Warren and Jack went to stay with their cousin on the outskirts of Dublin in a place called Dundrum.

"My goodness," said Jack in the drawing room one day. "There is a copy of my favourite book of all books, *Siegfreid and the Twilight of the Gods* illustrated by Arthur Rackham!"

"Do you really like the thing," said Warnie.

"I would give anything I have in order to purchase it, Warnie," said Jack. Fortunately Jack found a cheaper edition of the book available at 15 shillings.

"I'll give you help, Jack," said Warren.

"But you don't care for my interest in Norse mythology," answered Jack.

"No, it is true, it doesn't interest me very

much but you can have seven shillings and six pence towards the book. I'll give it to you gladly," said Warren out of sheer kindness for his brother.

It is important to understand in the story of this great storyteller that this book had a massive impact upon Jack's thinking. He had a natural ability to enter other worlds in his imagination and soon, of course, he was to create other worlds for millions of children to enter.

Jack, of course, began to adore the stories of the Norse Gods, in whom he did not believe. Sadly, the living God was still a stranger to him.

The time came in the Summer Term of 1913 for Jack to sit for the scholarship entrance examination to Malvern College. As it turned out he was extremely ill on the day of the examination with a high temperature. It was decided to allow him to attempt the examination in bed! Despite his illness and all the discomfort it brought, he won a Classical Entrance Scholarship.

"It was the finest achievement of his career," his brother Warren would always say. Jack was now poised to enter Malvern College and life under his headmaster 'Tubbs' was ending. He was very excited about the prospect and his hopes of a good time there were very high. They were hopes that were soon to be dashed.

Jack now felt the world
to be a very cruel place
and believed very strongly
that there was no God.

Misery upon Misery

Jack's first few days at his new school were spent in great anxiety. He had to find out what "Club" he belonged to for compulsory games. He absolutely hated games but ran anxiously to the main school building to try to search for his name on the notice board. Most of the other boys at the school, of course, just loved games and by the time he came near the notice board he noticed a huge crowd of boys milling around excitedly. Poor Jack could not get near enough to the board to see his name.

Realising he had better be back at his House soon, Jack ran back hoping to look for his name later.

"I say Lewis," said a boy standing at the door of the prefect's room as Jack ran past, "I can tell you the name of your Club. You and I are in the same one, it's B6!"

The boy was called Fribble and Jack was greatly indebted to him for his kindness and thanked him profusely. As time went by he went regularly to the notice board where the list for the

B Club was placed and was delighted that he never found his name on it thinking, of course, that he did not have to play. His delight did not last long because one day he discovered that B6 was not his Club at all. He had been tricked.

"Lewis," said a boy who had been sent to summon Jack before the assembled College prefects, "You are to be publicly flogged by the head of the College for the serious offence of skipping your Club." He then added sarcastically, "Who are you? Nobody," and rubbing salt into the wound he said, "Who is the Head of the College? The most important person there is."

Jack took his public flogging very bravely but it changed his whole attitude towards his school. He now had a deep sense of inferiority, feeling himself to be an outcast, an undesirable and clumsy boy. He was dreadfully lonely and very unhappy.

"But Lewis, this piece of translation from Horace is quite brilliant!" said Jack's Headmaster one day. For a fifteen year old the piece was just that. He had been placed in a High Form and excelled at school work. Strange as it may seem, school work was the one thing the fagging system of English Public Schools constantly interrupted. Fagging? This was a system by which senior pupils known at Malvern as Bloods called upon junior boys to do domestic work for them.

"Lewis!" a Blood would shout (how Jack used to hate his name being called) "Brush and polish my Officer's Training Corps kit!" "Lewis!

Clean out my study immediately!" "Lewis! Make my tea, now!"

The problem, of course, was that Jack had his work constantly interrupted by these calls. Day after day he had to wait in a queue of other boys at the "Boot hole" to get his turn at brushes and blacking in order to polish some senior boy's boots. The place was a cellar where it was dark, smelly and mostly freezing cold.

Picture then a boy closed in for thirteen long weeks with a society of other boys to whom games were the great goal and glory of life and that boy, hating games, and having to pretend that he loved them. Poor Jack! At House matches he had to shout with enthusiasm while all the time he detested it. Add to this the fact that Jack was growing very fast at this time and in all probability was outgrowing his strength. He later described himself as being "Dog-tired, cab-horse tired". He longed for night to come when he could get away from the whole miserable system and sleep.

Even then his nights were disturbed by constant toothache and he viewed the coming day with dread.

It was not, though, that this misery at Malvern College did not have its interruptions.

"Gotcha, Lewis!" the boy would cry as he rushed into Lewis' study with a gun in his hand. He was an eccentric Irish Earl who always carried a revolver. He would load one cylinder, point his revolver at a boy's head and count off before he

pulled the trigger! That boy's life depended on the
Earl's counting accurately! This pipe-smoking Earl
would go off at night on strange expeditions and
cared absolutely nothing for what counted as
success at Malvern College. In truth Jack was
constantly living between being shot in the head
and fagged out. Two things alleviated all of this
misery in Jack's life. One was called. 'The
Gurney', the nickname for the College Library
where, once a boy was inside he could not be
called out to fagg. He just loved sitting in the
library, his mind far away on his book. In the
summer term, from a glorious distance, there came
the sound of leather hitting wood. The cricket
match was, fortunately, in another world.

Fortunately too, at this time, Jack discovered
some other boys who shared his love of literature
and poetry. So, side by side, the two parts of his
life threaded their way through his time at Malvern
College. There was the dark and difficult side, his
deep hatred of the system of school life around
him and at the same time there was the inner joy
and pleasure he received from reading Norse,
Celtic, Greek and Roman mythology. He now felt
the world to be a very cruel place and believed
very strongly that there was no God.

At the end of his second term Jack wrote an
imploring letter to his father asking to be taken
away from the school.

"I am very sympathetic to what you have
written to me," said Albert Lewis when Jack came

home for the Easter holidays. "Warren and I, as you know, have been increasingly at loggerheads. He has been very surly and offhand with me. He resents my interest in knowing the details of his life. Malvern College has done very little for him."

Mr. Lewis, had, in fact, taken Warren away from Malvern and sent him to live with his own elderly retired Headmaster and his wife, Mr. and Mrs. Kirkpatrick who now lived at Bookham in Surrey. Mr. Kirkpatrick had been Headmaster of Lurgan College in County Armagh and was now preparing Warren for entry to Sandhurst, to become an Army Officer. Warren had made incredible progress through this gifted teacher.

"I could send you to Mr. Kirkpatrick in the autumn, Jack," said Mr. Lewis, gently. "He could coach you for an Oxford Scholarship. Life might be boring living with an elderly couple but it might be the very best thing for you at this time."

Jack couldn't believe what he was hearing. The whole idea was absolute bliss to him. To be able to study the subjects that he loved without Bloods calling on him to clean out their studies, polish their boots or make their tea! No more school games! Happiness beckoned. Freedom was only a term away.

"You shall have me
on a certain date, not before.
I will die in your wars if need be,
but till then I shall live my own life.
You may have my body
but not my mind."

C.S. Lewis prior to his recruitment
into the army in 1917

Happiness steps up

One day, just before Jack went back for his final
summer term at Malvern College, a message
arrived at 'Little Lea'. The message said that a boy
called Arthur Greeves, who lived nearby, was
convalescing in bed after an illness and would
welcome a visit from Jack. This boy had tried quite
a few times to make friends with Jack and Warren
but had been unsuccessful.

As it happened, Warren was, of course, at
Sandhurst and Jack, being alone, thought he would
go around and see Arthur. He arrived at his house
and climbed the stairs to his bedroom. Arthur was
sitting up in bed and on a table beside him lay a
book entitled, *Myths of The Norseman*.

"Do you like that?" said Jack.

"Do you like that?" said Arthur!

"Of course I do," replied Jack, and soon they
both discovered they had a deep love of Norse
mythology. By now they were almost shouting at
each other with excitement as they discovered
common ground between them. Jack simply

couldn't believe that he had found someone who shared the great passion of his life. He had found someone who understood him and sympathised with him.

"Let's read together," said Jack, "And compare notes."

They did more than that. They went on many walks together throughout the Holywood Hills in County Down. This was an area deeply loved by C. S. Lewis all of his life. Names like Stormont, Comber, Newtownards, Scrabo Hill, Craigantlet, Knocknagoney, all held a special magic for him.

In truth, the landscape of Narnia was the landscape of North Down. Here was a land of small fields, and many hedges. Dappled all across it was the gorse bush with its blazing yellow colour. There were abandoned quarries filled with water. Here the wind coming from the Irish Sea whistled through the grass and men following the plough were followed by screaming gulls. Jack could be picking mushrooms one moment and then moments later be looking down on the giant cranes of the Harland and Wolff shipyard. This was the shipyard where the RMS TITANIC had recently been built.

The landscape of Narnia, of course, was like the landscape of the Garden of Eden for Jack. The story of Narnia too was a representation of this. For C. S. Lewis the Holywood Hills were indeed his very own Garden of Eden!

Sadly, though, Europe was no Garden of

Eden as Jack returned home to Ulster on the Irish
Ferry after his last term at Malvern College.
Charlie Chaplain may have been making a big
name for himself in Hollywood and the tango was
all the rage in dancing that summer, but Europe
was a powder keg. Relations between nations were
breaking down at a frightening rate and Germany
increased its military budget by fifty percent. On
June 28th the heir to the Austrian-Hungarian
throne, the Arch Duke Franz Ferdinand and his
wife were travelling in a car through Sarajevo. A
bomb was thrown at them and landed in the seat of
their car. The Arch Duke coolly picked it up and
threw it away. Later that day a second attempt was
made to kill the Arch Duke and his wife. A
nineteen year old Bosnian student named Gavrilo
Trincep succeeded with another bomb. By August
17th 1.7 million men of eight nations were
engaged in a colossal European war, the size of
which had never been witnessed before in history.

Jack knew the time would soon come when
he would be of age to join up in the army.

"You shall have me," he said, "on a certain
date, not before. I will die in your wars if need be,
but till then I shall live my own life. You may have
my body but not my mind."

So it was that between 1914 and 1916 while
Europe erupted with ferocious warfare including
poison gas and 60,000 casualties fell at the Battle
of The Somme in one day alone, Jack Lewis came
into what proved to be one of the most contented

and happiest periods of his entire life. He once more boarded the Irish Ferry and headed down Belfast Lough for the open sea. Once more he arrived at Liverpool and took the train, this time to Waterloo Station and from there to Great Bookham in Surrey. All around him at the station soldiers were saying goodbye to their loved ones. He, though, was travelling to stay with a man who was to play one of the greatest influences on his life. As the woods, valleys and hills of Surrey, dotted with timbered houses with red-tiled roofs rushed past him, Jack wondered what Mr. Kirkpatrick, his new tutor, would be like.

On arrival at Great Bookham Station Jack found his tutor to be over six feet tall, with a moustache and side whiskers and he had an iron grip when he shook his hand.

"You are now proceeding along the principal artery between Great and Little Bookham," said Mr. Kirkpatrick as they walked away from the station. Jack, wondering what kind of a man he was going to have to deal with, began to make conversation with him.

"I was very surprised at the scenery of Surrey which I saw through my carriage window today," said Jack, sheepishly. "It was much wilder than I had expected."

"Stop!" shouted Mr. Kirkpatrick, making Jack jump. "What do you mean by wildness and what grounds had you for not expecting it?"

Jack suddenly realised that this man was not

trying to be cheeky, nor was he joking. He simply
wanted to know! He was a man who believed in
logic, that is reasoned thought or argument. If
somebody made a statement then he expected
them to be able to back that statement up. After a
few attempts. Jack realised that he had no real idea
why he used the word "wildness" to describe the
country-side of Surrey!

"Do you not see, then," said Mr. Kirkpatrick,
"that your remark is meaningless."

The conversation lasted for about three and a
half minutes but Jack soon discovered that that
was to be the direction of all conversations with
Mr. Kirkpatrick. Jack found out that Mr.
Kirkpatrick was ruthless in argument and
discussion. Soon Jack began to really enjoy
sparring with him in conversation. Mr. Kirkpatrick,
or 'The Great Knock', as the Lewis boys called
him, began in Jack a trait which would stay with
him all his life - the ability to argue on all kinds of
subjects with ruthless logic.

"Well, well, Mr. Kirkpatrick, it takes all sorts
to make a world," said a neighbour to 'The Great
Knock' one Sunday afternoon. "You are a Liberal
and I am a Conservative; we naturally look at the
facts from different angles."

"What do you mean?" said Mr. Kirkpatrick,
"Are you asking me to picture Liberals and
Conservatives playing peep-bo at a rectangular
fact from opposite sides of a table?".

The neighbour did not hurry into such

conversation as quickly again! The former Headmaster of Lurgan College had a favourite quotation which Jack always remembered. He would say, "You can have enlightenment for nine pence but you prefer ignorance."

"Excuse!" the Great Knock would say in the middle of a conversation. You knew when that word came, what you had just said was about to be set right.

It is a fascinating fact in the life of C. S. Lewis that the man who taught him logic was an atheist. It no doubt never crossed his mind that the sixteen year old boy he was now so brilliantly teaching was to turn out to be, arguably, the greatest Christian writer of the twentieth-century. Are not the ways of God, amazing? There can be no doubt that God used the training in logic in the mind of C. S. Lewis to help him write Christian truths so clearly in future years.

To any young person, Jack's life at Great Bookham would appear to be very boring. Yet, to Jack, it was absolute bliss. He later said that if he had his own way he would always live as he lived there. He had breakfast at 8 o'clock and was usually working at his desk by 9 o'clock with Mr. Kirkpatrick in a little study upstairs. The teaching was so good that Jack, for example, was soon thinking in Greek, never to speak of translating it!

"Elevenses, men!" said Mrs. Kirkpatrick as she brought the Great Knock and his pupil tea or coffee at 11 a.m.

"There's not a cup big enough to hold the tea I would like to drink, Mrs. Kirkpatrick," replied Jack with a smile. He loved to drink tea at any time! After the break Jack continued studying until one o'clock.

"Time for my walk, Mrs. Kirkpatrick!" Jack would say after lunch.

"You're going to know this countryside inside out, young Lewis," the Great Knock replied.

Jack then went walking through the afternoon and enjoyed being on his own, growing to love the valleys and villages, woods and hollows, field paths and lanes, dingles and copses, cottages, farmhouses, villas and the country houses of Surrey. Afternoon tea was at 4 o'clock and at 5 o'clock Jack returned to work again. He worked solidly through to 7 o'clock. Then came the evening meal and the time between that and bedtime was, he always maintained, for talk or a night out with friends. He believed in being in bed by 11 o'clock.

This quiet, scholarly and contented lifestyle at Great Bookham was occasionally interrupted by his brother Warren. He was now an officer in the British Army. When he came home, on leave from fighting in France, Warren would arrive in his young officer's uniform to take Jack back home to 'Little Lea' with him. They were no longer little boys sitting in a Liverpool Hotel, secretly puffing on their cigarettes and leafing through magazines as they waited for the ferry. Now Warren had money and bought first class railway tickets for them both and even the luxury of sleeping berths on the ferry. The young scholar and the young army officer were just as good friends as ever.

It is strange but true that great turning points in a person's life often hang on little events. One of those massive turning points in the life of C. S. Lewis was about to happen. Back in England on a cold autumn evening he stood on the long, timbered platform of Leatherhead Station in Surrey. He walked quite often to Leatherhead in order to have his hair cut and to look for books. That night he and one porter had the whole station platform to themselves. The hills beyond the station were almost violet in colour and the sky shimmered with frost. Dark was falling, and, as Jack walked the platform, idly, his ears tingling with the cold, he turned to the station bookstall and picked out a book in a dirty jacket, entitled, *Phantastes, a Faerie Romance* by George McDonald. As he held the book in his hand the train came in and the porter called out the names of the villages at which the train would be calling. "Bookham! Effingham! Horsley!" cried the porter.

"It's cold tonight", thought the sixteen year old Jack, as he stamped his feet on the platform, "I wish I was in my bed. Ah! Here comes the train!"

Soon after boarding the train Jack settled down in the corner and started to read the new book. George McDonald, who had been born near the Scottish town of Huntly in Aberdeenshire, had been a theologian, spiritual mystic, poet, novelist, preacher, scientist, essayist, highly successful lecturer, teacher, actor, editor and fantasy writer as well as a husband and the father of eleven children! He wrote over fifty books, thirty of them novels which sold millions of copies. Jack had never read one of his books before and now as the train rattled on through the dark autumn evening to Great Bookham, he found he simply could not put McDonald's book down.

"This book is terrific," thought Jack, "It is amazing how similar it is to the myths and legends that I love."

But it had more. It had hidden meaning. George McDonald was a follower of Jesus Christ and the underlining message in his book was what Jack later called the Voice of Holiness. Holiness is what God is. It means that God is lovely, pure, beautiful, infinitely good and precious, holiness is the very opposite of evil and God, who is holy, wishes all of us to be holy too. By trusting his Son Jesus Christ as Saviour we too can be made holy. Jack was a long way from understanding this message but suddenly be began to pick up the voice of God speaking through McDonald's novel which was an allegory of the spiritual pilgrimage out of this temporal world into the Kingdom of Heaven. Jack described the message of the book as being "like the voices which had called me from the world's end were now speaking at my side." He felt a deep desire to change, to be different. He

longed to, as he put it, "unmake myself". He was
slowly coming under conviction of the Holy Spirit
as to the need of what Jesus called a "new birth".
This is what the Lord Jesus can bring to any
person who trusts Him. He can completely change
that person's spirit and re-make them. Jack still
had a long way to go in his spiritual pilgrimage but
he said that a bright shadow had come out of the
book into the real world where he was and resting
there, transformed everything around him yet itself
remained unchanged. His imagination was deeply
touched by the book and soon millions through his
conversion to Christ were to be deeply influenced
toward the Christian faith themselves.

The train rolled on into the dark but Jack was
slowly rolling towards the Light.

The Story-teller

A few minutes after midnight
on Sunday, April 7th, 1918
some 2,500 muzzles roared in unison,
sending the first of what would be
30,000 shells towards
Armentieres
and filling the air
with mustard gas.

Into the trenches

One morning in the winter of 1916 snow began to fall on the fabled city of Oxford. It covered the wisteria that surrounded St. Edmund Hall and the tower of Magdalen College Chapel and the cobbled stones of Radcliffe Square. The College Quad was soon a carpet of white and the River Cherwell began to freeze.

A young Ulsterman in his great coat and muffler entered the Hall of Oriel to begin his Oxford University Scholarship Examination. It was so cold that he kept on his left-hand glove! Phelps, the Provost, handed out the papers. Jack began to write the essay that was before him. When it was all through he returned to Ireland telling his father that he felt almost certain that he had failed the examination. It was not so. By Christmas Eve Jack had learned he had been elected a scholar of University College.

Jack returned to the Great Knock for one last term to prepare for Responsions, a compulsory examination for all Oxford undergraduates, which included elementary mathematics.

"I cannot do mathematics, Mr. Kirkpatrick, I am simply hopeless at figures. I am sure I will fail Responsions."

"Come on Jack, we must try, you simply won't get into Oxford University without Responsions."

Sure enough when Jack eventually sat his Responsions exam, he failed it. It was to be an examination he never passed for after the first World War, a University Decree allowed ex-soldiers to be exempt from taking it. C. S. Lewis always said that if he had had to pass the examination he would have had to abandon any idea of ever going to Oxford.

As it turned out Jack took up residence in the summer term of 1917 at Oxford as a preliminary to going into the University Officer's Training Corps and was tutored by Mr. Campbell of Hertford College in Algebra in hope of passing his Responsions Examination!

While Jack was billeted at Keeble College he shared a room with a young cadet called Paddy Moore. They got on famously together.

"I have some leave coming up soon, Paddy," said Jack one day, "I think I will go home to Ireland."

"Why not come home and stay with me and my mother?" said Paddy, "You really would be very welcome."

"It really is very kind of you Paddy" said Jack, "I think I'll take you up on it."

He did, and, sadly, this showed that Jack was getting further and further away from his father. His father, unfortunately, did not seem to understand his son or his needs and even when Jack sent him a telegram in November 1917 asking that they meet in Bristol before he went overseas, Mr. Lewis, who really hated anything that disturbed his routine, wired a telegram back asking for a full explanation. It was too late. Jack had to sail for France and the Western Front without seeing his father. Jack was desperately disappointed that his father had not even bothered to come and see him. It was after all a very frightening moment in his life.

No Oxford University student really ever had a stranger first term. Half his college had been turned into a military hospital and about eight under-graduates lived in the other half. Jack did some regular military training and as soon as his first term was over he was commissioned as a Second Lieutenant in the Somerset Light Infantry and arrived in France on the day of his nineteenth birthday.

He had been travelling by night with three other officers in a very cold train from Rouen. The journey had lasted fifteen hours but as they were passing through a tunnel outside Rouen there came a very loud crash. Suddenly the door of their carriage dropped off into the darkness!

At the next stop a very angry Commanding Officer came in to speak to them.

"It is absolutely ridiculous that you men have been horseplaying."

"Horseplaying?" they said, thoroughly surprised.

"Yes! It is absolutely ridiculous that you have been playing around so much that you have pulled that door off yourselves."

Jack laughed it off as ridiculous as if four officers on a freezing winter's night would ever imagine to remove a carriage door even if they had been provided with screwdrivers!

On Jack's very first night in France he was taken into a huge marquee where about a hundred officers were to sleep on plank beds.

"You look rather lost, there!" said a Canadian Officer to Jack who did look rather bewildered in it all.

"Come on, we'll take charge of you and guide you through this lot" said another Canadian Officer. Jack was very glad to have friendly help in the midst of a strange new world.

Later, while eating alone at the Officer's Club at Arras two very senior officers came over to his table towards the end of his meal.

"Hello there 'Sunny Jim', come over to this corner with us." Jack looking at the red tabs and the ribbons on the officer's uniforms realised that these two men were very high-ranking officers indeed but that made no difference with Jack. They ordered him brandy and cigars and couldn't have been more kind to him.

But not all Jack's memories of the war are ones of friendship and cammeraderie. The scene that was unfolding before him was one of the most horrific the world has ever known. By March 1917 the Germans had three million soldiers on the Western Front. By August, General Hague's troops had poured four million rounds of ammunition from three thousand British guns towards the enemy lines. Unfortunately the rains were among the worst in thirty years and the water, having nowhere else to go, flooded the British trenches. Soldiers actually burdened by their heavy packs fell into shell holes brimming with water and drowned. In the fields of Flanders the poppies grew between the crosses, rows upon rows of them, that marked more than one hundred and fifty thousand fresh British graves after General Hague's offensive. The net gain was less than six miles of wasteland taken from the enemy. The battle of Passchendaele was a very costly thing.

Amazingly, during this nightmare Jack met lots of people who, like him, were scholars or poets. He met a delightful man called Johnston in his own Battalion. A scholar at Queen's College, Oxford, and a little older than Jack, they spent hours of discussion together. Johnston was moving towards a belief in God and deeply impressed Jack with his Christian ideals of truth and devotion to duty. Jack was sure that he had found a friend for life but, sadly, Johnston was killed.

In the midst of this ghastly life in the trenches, Jack developed trench fever. This brought him a very high temperature and he was sent for three weeks to a hospital at a little fishing village called Le Treport. To Jack it was sheer bliss. In comparison to the nightmare that was raging around him a bed and a book were to him the nearest thing to heaven he knew. The hospital was a converted hotel and Jack began, during those weeks, to read for the first time a volume of essays by the famous Christian writer, G. K. Chesterton. This was also used by God to draw him closer to Christian thinking.

Soon, though, Jack was back fighting in the trenches. He was just in time for the great final attack made by the Germans on the Western Front. Soon everything General Hague had won in his Passchendaele Drive was lost in a few days. The noise must have been horrendous. You could feel the impact as bomb after bomb exploded on impact with the muddy soil. The explosions, the tremors, the deafening noise were daily occurrences. One story Jack would tell from his war days showed how the awful business of war effected even the smallest of creatures. One day as Jack hid from German bullets in a muddy trench he saw something out of the corner of his eye. There, on the edge of a muddy puddle a little mouse sat shivering. The poor thing was terrified of Jack but it was too scared of all the noise and battle to run away - so it stayed by the puddle shivering. Jack moved his boot towards it but it did not have the courage to run away. He left it trembling by the puddle. Once Jack left, the mouse might pluck up the courage to move to a saver place. If a lull came in the fighting it might just survive. Jack carried on down the muddy trench, he never forgot that poor frightened animal.

"You OK Lieutenant?" said Sergeant Ayres to Jack day after day. Sergeant Ayres was known as Wallie to his friend. He was a farmer and was totally devoted to looking after his Lieutenant, Jack.

"Let me at those Germans" he would say, "Just let me at 'em!"

"I have never met a man anywhere like you, Sergeant," said Jack, "You are the only man I have ever met who really longs to fight."

"Just let me at 'em, Lieutenant," said Wallie.

By early April General Lundendorff moved his German troops to an incredible offensive. A few minutes after midnight on Sunday, April 7th, 1918 some 2,500 muzzles roared in unison, sending the first of what would be 30,000 shells towards Armentieres and filling the air with mustard gas.

Troops buckled on their coal-scuttle helmets, climbed over their parapets, and lurched across no-man's land. In the midst of all this offensive, Jack and Sergeant Ayres were fighting at a place called Arras. Suddenly, an English shell fell short and severely wounded Jack. Sadly, it killed Sergeant

Ayres who was standing just beside Jack. The Germans had been pouring shells into the British lines about three a minute all day.

Jack was carried from the trenches to hospital and his war was over. For the rest of his life his memories were to be troubled by all that he had gone through. Memories of going to sleep while marching and waking again and finding himself still marching. Memories of walking in the trenches in thigh gumboots with water above the knee and puncturing the gumboots on concealed barbed wire. He would remember how the icy water used to well up inside his boots. He never would forget the dead bodies that he constantly came across on battle fields and horribly smashed men which he described as "still moving like half-crushed beetles in landscape without a blade of grass".

There is nothing glorious about war. Even though people might today glorify people like the famous German Van Richthofen, "The Red Baron", who died in the same month in which Jack was wounded, there is nothing glorious about war. Nicknamed after his famous Fokker Triplane, Manfred Von Richthofen brought down eight enemy aircraft in two years. But, the truth is, he was at the start of a whole new area of warfare which was to be carried to the air in even deadlier form in the coming Second World War and further ghastly wars to follow it.

On the morning of November 11th, 1918 at 11:01 silence fell like a gentle mist on the

battlefields of Europe. The Germans signed an
Armistice at 5 a.m. and the ceasefire took effect
six hours later. The war was over, yet more than
eight million troops had died over its four year
history and over twenty-one million men were
wounded. In the last days of the war the Germans
had actually been recruiting fourteen year old boys
to fight in the German Army. They had run out of
manpower. People thought it was the war to end
all wars, but, sadly, they were wrong. The twenty-
one year old Jack, who resumed his studies at
Oxford University in January 1919, had come into
manhood through a nightmare.

"Come and see me,
I am homesick,
that is the long and short of it."

C.S. Lewis in a letter home

A Fellow at last

"That father of yours in Ireland," said one of
Jack's friends, "Is he a mythical creation or does
he really exist?"

"Come now," answered Jack, "He really does
exist but he just hates having his routine broken."

Jack could not have spoken truer words. He
wrote to his father from the London hospital
where he was gradually recovering from his
wounds. It was one of the most appealing letters
he had ever sent to anyone. It said:

"Wherever I am I know that you will come
and see me." Jack wrote to his father about how
he found it difficult to discuss personal matters, he
blamed it on his English school education and the
generation he had grown up in. But he continued
to plead with his father to come and visit him as he
needed him dreadfully at that time. Jack was home
sick for Ireland and for his father, whom he loved
dearly. Jack apologised for taking his father for
granted. His experiences of life had made him
realise how fortunate he was to have a father like

his. Jack promised to do better in the future and ended his letter with a further plea, 'Come and see me, I am homesick, that is the long and short of it."

His father never came. As Jack, who had now moved to a convalescent home near Bristol, wandered alone in its grounds he felt very sad. All around him he heard from the building the voices of relatives happy to be reunited with their sons after such a horrific war. He felt his father had let him down and didn't care about him.

One morning Jack, now getting back to robust health, set off for London to meet a very famous publisher who was going to publish a collection of his poems entitled, *Spirits in Bondage*. He found a stout little man with a bald head who was also fussy.

"Ah! Mr. Lewis!" said the publisher whose name was Heinemann, "I am so glad to meet you, have a seat."

"Good to be here, Mr. Heinemann," said Jack, glad to be seeing his life moving on to the things he cared about after the horror of war.

"You are doing very well, Mr. Lewis," he said with a smile. "The great writer and novelist, John Galsworthy who, of course, wrote the famous books called, *The Forsyte Saga*, wants to publish one of your poems in a new magazine."

"I am honoured," said Jack, quietly.

As Jack's health slowly returned he was at last able to return to Belfast. He decided to surprise his father and Warren who was already there. Taking the train and the old familiar ferry he slipped into Belfast and knocked on the door of 'Little Lea' on December 27th, 1918. He was rapturously welcomed.

"Let's drink champagne to your safe arrival home!" said Albert Lewis at dinner that evening. Despite Albert's inability to communicate at times with his sons it must never be forgotten that he loved them, deeply. 'Little Lea' echoed once more to animated and happy voices. The nightmare of a world war was receding and for those three men the pleasure of marking its end in their own family home could not have been happier.

"Ah!, Mr. Lewis!" said the porter in Jack's old College at Oxford. "You are most welcome back. I am glad you survived the war, Sir. It's just great to see you looking so well. Can I take you to your old room?"

Jack was delighted that the porter had recognised him. "Edwards!" said Jack on meeting an old friend, "This place is a much more agreeable place now."

It was just that. In fact Jack was once more overwhelmed with the beauty of the great University City. He loved it, and always would. Sadly though, at the first meeting of the Junior Common Room the minutes of the last meeting were read out, there were many names missing. The great war had left its ghastly mark.

Jack, at this time in his life, had struck up a relationship with his old friend Paddy Moore's mother. Jack and Paddy, the young cadet with whom he had shared a room at Keeble College, had, of course, made a promise before they had been called up to join the Army. It was a promise that if Jack was killed Paddy would care for the needs of Jack's father and if Paddy was killed Jack would care for the needs of Paddy's mother.

What had happened to Paddy? The Adjutant, who is the army officer in charge of routine administration filed a report. "He was last seen on the morning (of 24th March 1918) with a few men defending opposition on a river bank against infinitely superior numbers of the enemy.

"All the other officers and most of the men of his company have become casualties, and I fear it is impossible to obtain more definite information."

We are told that Mrs. Moore did learn later that Paddy was taken prisoner, overthrew his guards and got back to the British Army lines. He was then sent back "over the top". "Over the top" was an expression used in the First World War to describe an infantry attack by either side as it involved soldiers climbing the banks of their trenches and facing murderous fire as they tried to capture new ground.

Paddy Moore was hit in the leg and as he lay in a field, his batman tried desperately to staunch the flow of blood. A batman is an officer's servant in the armed forces. Disastrously, as the batman did his best to save Paddy, a bullet tore through Paddy's head, killing him instantly.

The Story-teller

From the summer term of 1919 Jack lived with Mrs. Moore and her daughter Maureen in rented houses in Oxford for eleven years. His father was not at all pleased and Warren was not too happy with Mrs. Moore, either. He wrote a very bitter description of her;

"A woman of very limited mind, and notably domineering and possessive by temperament." Warren complained that she commandeered most of Jack's time reducing the number of visits he could make to his father. Warren despised her constant interfering with Jack's work. Warren also accused her of being bone idle and giving Jack endless domestic duties and chores to do. These in Warren's opinion took up too much of Jack's time. Warren did not appreciate Mrs. Moore at all and believed her to be selfish and ignorant. He cheerfully pointed out that he had never, in twenty years seen a book in her hands and that her main topic of conversation was always herself. But perhaps Warren's main grievance with Mrs. Moore was the demand she made on Jack's meagre allowance which was calculated to suit a bachelor living in College and certainly not a householder with dependants. Jack found himself miserably poor.

This is true to an extent. It is true that poor Jack did have to do a lot of chores. He wrote in his journal:

"Got up shortly before seven, cleaned the grate, lit the fire, made tea, "did" the drawing-room, made toast, bathed, shaved, breakfast, washed up, put the piece of ham on to boil, was out by half past ten ... washed up after lunch."

Yet, was it all as bad as Warren said? In the end, it wasn't. Jack called Mrs. Moore "Mother" and there is no question that she was very kind to him. "She was generous and taught me to be generous," Jack later stated to his friend George Sayer, "If it were not for her, I should know little or nothing about ordinary domestic life as lived by most people. I was brought down to earth and made to work with my hands."

Out of this experience Jack was able to write about everyday life in a way many secluded academics could never do. Millions, particularly children, were to benefit as a result.

At University his life flourished. He had around him friends of great wit and brilliance. He argued and talked with them all. They were to influence him deeply and challenge his own beliefs.

"Jack, never forget to absorb the atmosphere of any place you might find yourself," said his friend A. Hamilton Jenkin, "You can find beauty and grandeur even in the grimness and squalor of an industrial town. Seek value in all things." Jack learnt this truth quickly and was one day to make even an old wardrobe into something extraordinary. He was also delighted to have the friendship of A. C. Harwod and Owen Barfield of whom Jack said, "Barfield cannot talk on any subject without illuminating it."

"You will be all right! Calm down!" cried Jack as he struggled to hold down a friend of his with whom he was spending a couple of weeks.

"Hell! Devils!" the man screamed. Sadly he was going mad. He had dabbled in the occult and Jack was shocked by what he heard. Jack had been warned and his love of speculation about the subject of the occult was reined in.

He did not have a lot of money at this time in his life. Providing for three people, himself, Mrs. Moore and her daughter Maureen, led him to acute poverty. His University scholarship and his father's allowance were just not enough. He began to have headaches, suffered from indigestion and found it very hard to sleep at night. Panic caught him. He wondered if he would ever accomplish his great desire to write great works.

In 1922 Jack did brilliantly in his final examination results. He came first in Classics and Philosophy. But his brilliance did not provide him with a University post, although he tried for several. He was advised to stay on at Oxford for a fourth year to study English Literature as it was felt this would put him in a strong position for future University posts. His scholarship from the University could be renewed for the year and he was asked if he could afford to stay. He wrote to ask his father's advice.

"Now if," he wrote, "you feel that the scheme is rather a tall order and that my education has already taken long enough, you must frankly tell me so." Fortunately for Jack Mr. Lewis gave him the financial support he needed and Jack was extremely grateful to him. He thoroughly enjoyed his year studying English Literature and Language and he wrote very enthusiastic letters to his father describing what he was experiencing. He even had to learn the Anglo Saxon language and found it fascinating.

During this year of study Jack drew close to his friend Neville Coghill from County Cork in Ireland. He was a tall, handsome man with a brilliant mind and a charming manner. He studied English through the year with Jack. They went for many walks together over the Cumnor Hills arguing, agreeing and disagreeing as they talked of the books they had been reading the week before.

Jack was greatly shocked to find that his friend Neville was a convinced Christian. He also began to discover that the authors who meant most to him in his reading were also Christians.

The writer George McDonald had begun it all. The poems of the great John Donne, Dean of St. Paul's Cathedral in London in the seventeenth-century, he said, intoxicated him. The poems also of the country parson, George Herbert who died in 1632, also touched Jack deeply. The atheistic writers that he had read did not grip him as the Christians did and he began to say, "Christians are wrong, but all the rest are bores." Jack was still an atheist and maintained that Christianity was only a myth.

At the end of the year Jack gained a First in English. This was a very great achievement and he now had a Double First which was a great qualification for a future post.

In May 1924 relief came. A Philosophy tutor at University College was going to America for a year and Jack was invited to take his tutoring when he was away. A tutor is a person who teaches individuals or small groups at a university. He was also asked to give lectures during the year. He took the offer immediately.

Jack gave fourteen lectures that term and earned more money in grading examination papers on English Literature for the Oxford and Cambridge University Examination Board. Then his fortune really turned. He applied to teach English at Magdalen College and thought he hadn't a hope. He was wrong. On May 20th a telegram announcing that he had been elected reached his father.

"Elected Fellow Magdalen. Jack," it read.

His father wrote in his diary: "I went to his room and burst into tears of joy." Then Jack's father knelt down on the floor of his son's room at 'Little Lea' and thanked God from the bottom of his heart. Albert Lewis' prayers for his son's future had been heard and answered.

So Jack was now a Fellow? What's that I hear you ask. A Fellow is not only a teacher at a university but he is also a member of the governing body of the college where he teaches. Jack was now set to teach both English and Philosophy and his period of poverty ended. His good friend, George Sayer, has pointed out that the poverty Jack had known marked him for the rest of his life. He states that Jack found it difficult to spend more than the minimum amount on himself or more than a necessary amount on anyone or anything. He gained complete freedom from the snobbery that people have because of what they possess and he also had a deep sympathy with and an understanding of poor people. In future years he was to give many thousands of pounds to people who were short of money.

However, little did Jack know that he was about to experience a possession of the greatest wealth any person can ever know: the spiritual wealth that comes from a personal knowledge of the Lord Jesus. It was not only to change his life, it was to change his destiny.

The Story-teller

In the Trinity Term of 1929 I gave in,
and admitted God was God,
and knelt and prayed:
perhaps that night,
the most dejected
and reluctant convert
in England.

C.S. Lewis on his conversion

A Light from beyond the world

It was August 1929 and Jack now found himself back in Belfast caring for his father, Albert, who was not feeling at all well. For ten days he busily saw to his father's needs at 'Little Lea', shaving him, reading to him and even sharing a humorous story or two from Oxford to try to cheer him up. Jack always had a delightful streak of humour in his personality.

"Did you hear the one about the Professor from Leeds University, father?", he asked.

"What about him?", said Albert grinning.

"Well", said Jack warming to his story, "This professor sat in a railway carriage. Opposite him a middle aged woman was fidgeting anxiously. She was worried about what he was carrying in a perforated cardboard box on top of his lap. Eventually she could stand it no longer and plucked up the courage to ask the professor about his peculiar package.

'If you don't mind me asking' she said nervously, 'What is inside your box, sir?'

'A mongoose, madam', replied the Professor.

Surprised the lady continued her inquisition

'And what do you plan to do with the mongoose Sir?'

'I will take it to a friend of mine who is, unfortunately, suffering from the dreadful disease delirium tremens.'

The woman looked quite alarmed and then she continued. 'What use will the mongoose be to him?'

'Why, madam,' the professor replied indignantly, 'the people who suffer from that particular disease, delirium tremens, actually find themselves surrounded with snakes.'

The woman squealed before adding, 'My goodness!'

The Professor continued, 'And, of course, a mongoose eats snakes.'

Grimacing the woman continued to quiz the professor, 'But you don't mean that the snakes are real?' she exclaimed.

'Oh, dear me, no,' replied the Professor. 'The snakes aren't real but then, of course, neither is the mongoose!'"

They all had a good laugh at that one!

When Jack wasn't with his father he would roam through the halls and rooms of 'Little Lea' opening the windows that his father had always kept closed. He sat alone in the dining room eating a few biscuits and fruit, recalling the days when he had eaten huge compulsory meals there at mid-day.

"Come on, Jack, you need a good walk," said Arthur Greeves who visited 'Little Lea' every day.

"I'll go for an hour," said Jack glad to be free for a while from the way the house was taking him back in his mind and spirit to the pleasures and pains of his childhood. When his father had settled for the night Jack went out into the garden. He enjoyed the cool air which was in contrast with the stuffy air of the sick room and he stood there listening to the frogs croaking in the field at the bottom of the garden.

Albert's pain persisted and Jack's cousin, Dr. Joseph Lewis, recommended that Albert had an operation. He was put into Miss Bradshaw's nursing home. Jack remained at home visiting his father every day. The operation discovered cancer.

"We think he might live a few years," the doctors told Jack.

One day as Albert's mind wandered under sedatives, he suddenly turned to his son and asked:

"What do you remember of your mother's death?"

"Not much," replied Jack, "I remember her giving Warren and I a Bible each a few days before she died. I remember crying out to her one night when I had toothache but she didn't come. I was told later that she had cancer but beyond that I knew nothing."

Albert then began to speak to Jack of his wife's death. He told him how he had held his wife's hand and listened to her as she wandered in

and out of the anaesthetics they had given her.
Some Orangemen had been beating their drums for
hours not far from her window and she had said,
"It's a pity that it takes so long to learn that tune."

"When you get married," she had said to a
nurse attending her, "see that you get a good man
who loves you and loves God."

"What have we done for Him?" she had asked
Albert as she had talked with him of spiritual
things as she was dying. It was a very penetrating
question. Flora Lewis was not to know in this life
that her little boy was to be so mightily used by
God in the coming days of the twentieth century
and beyond.

"I shall have to return to Oxford, Michaelmas
Term is approaching," said Jack quietly to his
father in mid-September.

Dr. Joseph Lewis had told Jack that things
might not change for weeks in his father's
condition either for better or for worse. Jack left
Belfast on Saturday, September 22nd. There must
have been very sad thoughts in his mind as he
sailed on the ferry down Belfast Lough. The
relationship between Jack and his father had not
always been a happy one. He had at times deceived
his father and spoken negatively about him and
Jack now felt ashamed of this.

Nevertheless, they had drawn close over the
past week. This was fortunate because Jack was
not to have another opportunity to heal the
relationship. On the following Tuesday he received

a telegram telling him that his father was now gravely ill. He left Magdalen within the hour, caught the Liverpool ferry and arrived at Miss Bradshaw's nursing home the following morning. It was too late. Jack's father had passed away on the Tuesday afternoon.

On September 27th 1929 a cable arrived at the Army Service Corps Headquarters, North China Command, for Warren Lewis. It read, "Sorry, report father dead, painless, 25th September. Jack." Warren sat down and immediately composed a letter to his brother.

A lot of letters passed between Warren and Jack over the next month as they grieved, shared memories from the past and planned for the future. It was April 1930 before Warren could return to England from China. Towards the end of the month he and Jack returned to Belfast together. They immediately visited their father's grave and then took a taxi to 'Little Lea' where Mary Cullen, the cook and housekeeper for the past thirteen years, greeted them at the door and served them lunch. They then set about organising what they wanted shipped from the house to Oxford, including carpets and books.

"Ah, Warnie, we really had better destroy our trunk of childhood toys, don't you think?" said Jack.

"Well, we did agree by letter that we would do it," said Warren. "How do you think we should destroy them?"

"Let's bury the trunk in the vegetable garden," said Jack.

It was a rare sight as the two grown men dragged the trunk of their childhood toys down to the vegetable garden at 'Little Lea', now hugely overgrown. They then started to dig a hole.

"Should we have one last look?" asked Jack thinking of the stuffed animals and china figures that they had used as children to populate the imaginative world they had created. Together they decided to let bygones be bygones and bury the trunk unopened.

"How did we create so much out of so little?" they mused as they filled in the hole. Jack didn't bury his memories, though. The imagination that had fired his own childhood would, by his pen, soon fire the imagination of millions of other childhoods. For now, though, it was back to Oxford.

Interestingly, when Warren came back from China Jack discovered his brother was thinking about becoming a Christian.

"Let's go to Church together," said Warren.

"Agreed," said Jack. "Though I have to say that I feel that it is a time-wasting exercise. The fuss! The bells! The crowds! The umbrellas! The notices! The bustle! All that arranging and organising! I think it would be better if people prayed alone or met in twos or threes to talk about spiritual things. And to be honest, Warnie, I do not like hymns, either."

The truth was that Jack, at this stage, was not a Christian. He was slowly coming to believe that there was a God, or Spirit, behind the Universe but he did not think it possible to have any personal relationship with him.

Through these years Jack felt isolated by a very powerful group of people who dominated university politics, particularly at Magdalen College. Jack had been elected a Fellow at Magdalen for a five year contract but in actual fact his post lasted for twenty-nine years. But because he felt so isolated Jack felt it might be a good idea to call some of his close friends together for weekly meetings where he could encourage them in their writing careers. Quite a few of them were outstanding writers. He wanted to provide a place where they could simply enjoy each other's company in the tough environment of Magdalen College.

"What shall we call these meetings, Jack?" said one of his friends, one day.

"'The Inklings!'" he replied, and 'The Inklings' they became.

"And when shall we meet?"

"Thursdays, at my rooms," answered Jack, "the meetings are to be informal with no rules, no officers, and no set order to discussions."

"How does one become a member?" someone asked.

"All who come have to be invited by me!" said Jack.

"Well, I'm glad you put me on your list," said Professor J. R. R. Tolkien. The friendship between C. S. Lewis and Tolkien became one of the most important literary friendships of the 20th century. In later years Tolkien would read the newest chapter from his book, *Lord of the Rings* or *The Silnarillion* or *The Hobbitt* for he too was a superb storyteller.

Other friends soon joined the circle and would read their work to each other. Professor Coghill, David Cecil, Roy Campbell, all men of intellectual brilliance, poured out their wit, arguments and judgment at the meetings of 'The Inklings'. They also used to meet on Tuesdays in the back room of a pub called 'The Eagle and Child' for an hour or two before lunch.

"Ah! Mr. Lewis," said the publican.

"So your 'lot' are due again?"

"I'm afraid so, Mr. Blagrove, we're a hard lot to get rid of!"

"Not like the autocratic lot I used to serve," said the hearty publican who had previously been a cab driver in Oxford.

"What do you mean?" asked Jack.

"Why, I used to drive people in my cab that were so fussy they would have given me their suits if they did not fit properly! Those were the days when they also used to hire my cab to take them somewhere 'where they could find a fight.'"

There was no fighting in the back room of 'The Eagle and Child' except of the intellectual kind. And there was plenty of that. Jack loved his friends and they enjoyed their times together as a relaxation from the hard work of tutoring, lecturing and writing. Not all conversations, though, amongst these friends, were about their literary work. On September 19th, 1931 Lewis dined at the Hall of Magdalen College. Dinner there was always an occasion. At one end was a seventeenth-century screen carved with scenes from the life of Mary Magdelene and above it was a choir's gallery. At the other end was a low raised platform which ran right across the entire width of the room on which sat the high table, made of English oak.

The Fellows, who are members of the governing body of the college, would meet for a drink in the Senior Common Room while undergraduates and other members of the College would take their places for dinner at the Hall. They would remain standing while the Fellows entered the room in procession wearing their black gowns, while undergraduates wore little gowns like sleeveless jackets without buttons. Grace would be said in Latin by the President, Vice President or Senior Fellow of the College and the meal would begin. Later wine would be taken in the Common Room with nuts and fruit eaten with silver fruit knives and forks.

"How are you, Lord Adrian?" said C. S. Lewis to the Great Nobel Prize Winner, famous for his work on pain and nerve cells.

"All the better for this good food, Mr. Lewis."

"And Professor Taylor, how are you?"

"Fine C. S., how's your science fiction novel coming on? What's its title?"

'*Out of the Silent Planet* A.P.J ... Good evening, Lord David," said Jack as he moved to another piece of fruit.

On September 19th, 1931 after dinner Jack and two friends, Tolkien and Dyson were strolling round Addisions Walk in Oxford, discussing the truth of the Gospels and how Christ died.

"Christ dying can transform all who believe on Him," said Tolkein.

"But what bearing does such a story have on my life?" asked Jack.

"To find out its relevance to your life, Jack, you must plunge in!" replied Tolkien.

The conversation developed deeper and deeper until the clock struck 3 a.m!

"I must go home to my wife," said Tolkien. Dyson stayed on talking with Jack.

"Christianity works for the believer," said Dyson.

"Really Hugo?"

"Yes, of course. You will have peace with God and the forgiveness of your sins."

"What about my faults and my sins?" asked Jack.

"Christ will help you overcome your faults and give you power to resist sin. You will become a new person."

Slowly, C. S. Lewis was moving towards the most momentous experience of his life. One day in 1929 he had been sitting on the top deck of a bus when he suddenly was aware that he was holding something back, shutting something out of his life. He knew he was facing a door which he could keep shut or go through. He said he was like a man of snow who after being frozen and stiff for a very long time had started to thaw.

"The melting was starting in my back, drip, drip and presently trickle, trickle." He knew that God was moving in on him asking for total surrender.

"You must picture me alone in that room at Magdalen, night after night", he wrote later, "Feeling... the steady unrelenting approach of Him whom I so earnestly desired not to meet ... In the Trinity Term of 1929 I gave in, and admitted God was God, and knelt and prayed: perhaps that night, the most dejected and reluctant convert in England. I did not see then what is now the most shining and obvious thing; the divine humility which will accept a convert even on such terms."

Jack was no longer an atheist but he was not yet a Christian, a believer and follower of Jesus Christ. He believed in God and he went to church but the conversation with Tolkein and Dyson had a profound effect upon him. Twelve days later he and Warnie decided to visit Whipsnade Zoo.

"Let's go on my motorcycle," said Warnie, "You can travel in the side car."

Imagine the great Oxford scholar and his brother setting out for London on that motor cycle and side car on that sunny morning. It ended, in fact, in one of the most important journeys in the twentieth-century: the journey of C. S. Lewis to Christian conversion.

Jesus once said to a great academic called Nicodemus: "Unless one is born again, he cannot see the Kingdom of God". Nicodemus then asked Him, "How can a man be born when he is old? Can he enter a second time into his mother's womb and be born?" Jesus answered, "Do not marvel that I said to you, ' You must be born again. The wind blows where it wishes and you hear the sound of it but cannot tell where it comes from and where it goes. So is everyone who is born of the Spirit.'"

Jack's experience on that sunny morning describes exactly what Jesus told Nicodemus was vital for anyone who wants to become a Christian. Later, describing what happened, Jack wrote:

"When we set out I did not believe that Jesus Christ is the Son of God and when we reached the Zoo I did."

"He who believes that Jesus Christ is the Son of God is born of God," wrote the Apostle John in the Scriptures. So it was for C.S. Lewis. The great storyteller was on his way to communicate the greatest story ever told.

The Story-teller

"When we set out
I did not believe
that Jesus Christ
is the Son of God
when we reached the Zoo
I did."

C.S. Lewis on his conversion

The Devil at work

One day in July 1930 Warnie and Jack found a house in a beautiful area, three miles from the centre of Oxford.

"It's lovely," said Warnie, looking around.

"It even has a wood!" said an excited Jack in his loud booming voice. Half of the property was a wooded segment of Shotover Hill.

"Look, an orchard!" said a delighted Warnie.

"And a tennis court!" chorused Jack.

Between the higher and lower ground of the property was a large pond.

"It used to be a pit from which clay was dug for brick-making," said the estate agent.

"Over here are the kilns in which the bricks were fired," he continued, "They are in ruin now covered by that ivy and I'm afraid a lot of weeds."

"I really like it," said Jack as they travelled back to Oxford along the long, pot-holed, driveway of Kiln Lane that led to the house.

"It's out in the country and yet so near your work Jack."

"And near church, too," said Warnie, knowing that the village of Headington Quarry where they attended church was only half a mile away.

'The Kilns' and eight acres of land were bought for £3,300, of which Jack paid £1,500. The house was bought in Mrs. Moore's name and was legally hers. She left a will which stated that if she died the house belonged to Jack and Warnie for their lifetime. In fact, 'The Kilns' was the real home of C.S. Lewis for the rest of his life.

"You mean you swim in that dirty pond most mornings before breakfast?" people would say to Jack in surprise.

"I do indeed," he would reply, "It looks dirty but I can tell you I come out perfectly clean".

"And how do you enter the pool?"

"From a punt which I push out from under the trees over there into the open water. I constantly disturb the moorhens and their chicks!"

Coming to know Christ seemed to open up huge creativity in the life of C. S. Lewis. Books started to pour out of him. *Out of the Silent Planet* came in 1938, the first of his three science fiction stories. "Terrifying and beautiful," wrote one critic, "Brilliantly imagined and exciting," said *The Times* of London, pointing out that the book, they reckoned, had been used to "convey a deep conviction about God and about living."

More books were to come, *The Problem of Pain, Mere Christianity, The Screwtape Letters,*

Perelandra, and *That Hideous Strength*, part of the space trilogy, *The Great Divorce; A Dream*, *Miracles*, *Till we Have Faces*, *Reflections on the Psalms*, *The Four Loves*, and *The Seven Chronicles of Narnia*.

Articles and eventually BBC broadcasts, speeches, books: what kind of discipline did the man have to be able to do all these things? How did he order his day? Let's take a typical day when during the university term he stayed at his rooms in Magdalen College. It makes interesting reading.

5.30 a.m.	Prayers and Bible Reading. He would then make himself a cup of tea.
7.15 a.m.	Called by the college scout and served a cup of tea. Bathed and shaved. A brief walk, praying, praising God, and contemplating beauty of nature.
8.00 a.m.	College Chapel for Dean's prayers. Breakfast with other worshippers in Common Room.
8.45 a.m.	In his Oxford Rooms, opening letters and notes and trying to answer them.

9.00 a.m.	Students came every hour, except on Mondays, and on days when he lectured in buildings on Oxford's High Street.
1.00 p.m.	Be taken by Maureen Moore or Fred Paxford (Handyman and Gardener at 'The Kilns') for lunch at 'The Kilns'.
1-1.45 p.m.	Spend time digging or sawing in the woods at 'The Kilns', or with a friend, go for a brisk walk.
4.45 p.m.	Drive back to Magdalen College and lecture or receive students.
7.15 p.m.	Dinner at Magdalen College Hall.
7.15-11 p.m.	Tuesday Night's pupils would come to read the great Anglo-Saxon saga of Beowulf with him from 8.30 p.m.

Other evenings there would be meetings at the College Literary Society and invitations to dine at other Colleges. Invitations he would return, etc. By the time Lewis fell into bed at 11 p.m. in his quiet college bedroom he desperately needed

sleep! On Mondays he had no pupils at all and
spent his time preparing lectures and correcting
work done and reading. Saturday he had no pupils
after 1 p.m. and often went for country walks.

In December 1931, the year after his
conversion, Jack became a full practising member
of the Church of England. He received
Communion on Christmas Day at the Church at
Headington Quarry. It was the first time he had
taken it since childhood when he had been
confirmed but was not a true believer at the time, a
fact of which he was ashamed.

The next nine years passed in what Jack
described to his friend Owen Barfield as a "corker"
of a time but slowly the shadow of coming war
began to loom on the horizon.

"The Jews have made no contribution to
human culture," Adolf Hitler had pronounced,
"and in crushing them I am doing the will of the
Lord." He became Chancellor of Germany in
January 1933 and by the end of the year he was
burning books, beating workers and, tragically,
murdering Jewish people. In November of that
year Jack wrote to his friend Arthur Grieves:

"That blaspheming tyrant has just fixed his
absurdity for all to see in a single sentence and
shown that he is as contemptible for his stupidity
as he is detestable for his cruelty."

Jack had known all about the horror of war
and now dreaded the possible separations and
disasters that were looming.

In September 1939 war was declared with Germany and millions of lives were affected. 'The Kilns' was blacked out, as were all other houses in Oxford, because, of course, light would give German air bombers a view of the city.

"Let's put up our house for use by evacuees," said Jack to Mrs. Moore one day. The news had spread of a desperate need for houses to be put at the disposal of children evacuated from London and other cities. These children were in danger from German bombing.

"Agreed," said Mrs. Moore. "Are you sure you don't mind the disruption to your work, Jack? Children are noisy, you know, and you need peace to study and write."

"Not at all," said Jack. "We may save quite a few children's lives and what's more, they will be a lot of fun."

The day they arrived Jack was touched by how much the school girls sent to 'The Kilns' seemed to love their new surroundings.

"Cor, Mr. Lewis," said one girl, "you have even got two swans on your lake".

"Given to me as a gift by the Provost of Worcester College," said Jack with a smile.

"Don't reckon anybody would ever give me two swans for a present!" she replied.

"They tend to stay away from me when I swim in the pond in the mornings," said Jack.

"You swim in the pond?" the girls chorused.

"I do indeed," replied Jack.

The schoolgirls loved 'The Kilns' and its seclusion and particularly its orchard and tennis court. They ate the delicious plums and dozens of different sorts of apples and pears that Paxford the gardener had grown.

They played endlessly in the woods where Jack and Warnie had within the space of about one year actually had forty-three new trees planted.

They were also full of questions when they discovered what C. S. Lewis did and as they walked with him in the city or ate with him at meals, the questions poured out.

"How old is the College you work in?"

"It was founded by William of Waynflete in 1458 on the West Bank of the River Cherwell."

"What's the May Day Choir?"

"Oh! That's the Magdalen College Choir (pronounced Maudlen) who go up to the top of the Magdalen Bell Tower at five o'clock each May Day morning. When the sun rises they sing a Latin hymn to the Holy Trinity. They have been doing that since the Tower was completed in 1504!

"When were women allowed into Oxford?"

"They weren't allowed full membership until 1920!"

"Shame on Oxford!"

"What's an undergraduate, Mr. Lewis?"

"That's the name of a student who hasn't finished his or her course and taken their degree."

"What's a degree, Mr. Lewis?"

"That's an award given by a university or

college when a student successfully completes their course."

"They say you're a Fellow of Oxford, Mr. Lewis, what's a Fellow?"

"A Fellow is sometimes called a Don and is chosen from graduates who are going on to valuable studies of their own and who help with the teaching of undergraduates."

"You're also a tutor, Mr. Lewis, what's that?"

"A tutor is a supervisor of studies. That is someone who watches over, directs or checks a student's work. Once a week the undergraduate at Oxford goes to see his or her college tutor to talk about the books read, to read out essays the tutor has given to write and to discuss any problems."

"Do you like your work, Mr. Lewis?"

"Love it!" he replied.

In the spiritual journey of C. S. Lewis the influence of those London children can't be valued. It was priceless! Jack was actually very shy of children and even ignorant of their ways but these young evacuees opened up a whole new world to him and out of it all God used the experience to lead him to write the Narnia stories. The children fired his imagination.

"Isn't this war awful?" people would say to Jack.

"Indeed it is, but at least petrol rationing means fewer cars on the street so I can walk them better! Blackening out of houses means I can also see Oxford by moonlight!" he would answer.

"Is there anything to help the war effort that I can do?" Jack asked at the Recruiting Office, one day, "I would like to volunteer to be an instructor of cadets."

His offer was not accepted but they did suggest he work for the Ministry of Information. "Don't want to do that," said Jack, "I would have to write lies in the newspapers to fool the Germans as part of my work and I would much rather serve in the Home Guard."

He did, and it must have amused many who knew him to see such a great scholar and writer walking through Oxford at 1.30 a.m. to start his stint of duty at the Home Guard centre. Every Saturday morning, very early you would see him walking along munching his sandwiches. No one would have guessed he was an Oxford Don in real life.

"Evening Mr. Lewis," chorused the two cheerful young men who shared his spell of duty. They would then hand him his rifle.

The Home Guard was a body of part-time soldiers who were recruited to repel any German troops that might land from the air. They have now, of course, been made very famous by a BBC TV series called "Dad's Army".

At dawn he walked home through Oxford as the sun began to slowly rise upon the city and got to his bed at five in the morning.

Through this time with many schoolgirls in his home, a rifle over his shoulder on moonlit nights, building a dug-out for protection from air-raids in the garden, sawing logs for the fires in his home, Jack's mind was still very busy. He was conceiving a book which he wrote during the autumn and winter of the war called *The Problem of Pain*. Of all his books it became one of the most popular. It sets out to show very powerfully that the Christian faith has a lot to say to those who suffer. It brought great comfort to war-time readers.

"Warnie," said Jack on returning from church one morning, "I was listening to the Rev. Bleiben in church this morning and I was struck with an idea during the sermon for a book."

"And pray tell me, Jack, what will you call it?"

"From One Devil to Another."

"Goodness, you have been struck by an idea, brother! What on earth form will it take?"

"Well, Warnie, it will be a book of letters of advice from an elderly devil to a young one who has just started out on his young patient to try and convince him that the doctrines of the Christian faith are the sort of thing that can't really be true!"

"A devil of a book that would be, Jack!" said Warnie.

Those letters of course, became known as *The Screwtape Letters* which have now sold at least two million copies worldwide! They are a most original way of showing the distinction between good and evil and how that it is possible, by God's strength, to become good. One thing is certain, the Devil was busy across Europe in the slaughter of millions as the war progressed and it was wonderful how C. S. Lewis was used by God to bring people to faith and the truth of the Bible. He was about to be used, though, in a way he had not yet imagined.

"Keep nothing back.
Nothing that you have not
given away
will ever really be yours ... "

C.S. Lewis, Mere Christianity

Talking to millions

"Right and wrong: a clue to the meaning of the Universe," said *The Radio Times*. Every Wednesday during August 1941 a fifteen minute talk was given on the BBC from London. What was this? It was certainly a fascinating subject. The speaker was C. S. Lewis. The director of Religious Broadcasting at the BBC, Dr. James Welsh, had been touched and inspired by Jack's book called *The Problem of Pain* and felt Jack would make a great religious broadcaster. He was right.

"Listen to this bloke!" said the bar tender, turning up the radio in a pub filled with soldiers, "He's really worth listening to." They listened closely and with full attention for the entire broadcast.

All over the United Kingdom people's attention was captured by Jack's rich, down-to-earth voice that talked of faith and hope, sin and forgiveness and the Christian view of God. Compelling, logical, and brilliant, millions of people listened in to some of the most powerful religious broadcasting of the twentieth-century. People's lives were darkened by war and hopelessness and Jack's broadcast brought them meaning and purpose. People were compelled to listen by the very way Jack spoke. Imagine listening to these soaring, moving words of Jack on radio in those frightening days:

"Give up yourself, and you will find your real self. Lose life and you will save it... submit with every fibre of your being and you will find eternal life ... look to Christ and you will find Him and with Him everything else is thrown in."

Perhaps one of the most famous challenges Jack Lewis ever threw out to non-Christians came in one of his BBC talks entitled, *The Shocking Alternative*. He asked if Jesus was a good man and a good moral teacher, even a great one? Or was He, as He claimed, the Son of God? C. S. Lewis said that the only options available when considering who Jesus Christ was were that he was either a "lunatic - on a level with a man who says he's a poached egg - or the Devil of Hell". Jack then threw out his powerful challenge: "Either this man was, and is, the Son of God: or else a madman: or something worse." Jack insisted that people had to make a choice. They still do.

On July 19th, 1943 Jack took part in a programme called, *The Anvil*. An interviewer asked Jack 'Do you not believe that the Bible is partly fiction, that is, a story made up by writers like novels or legends.'

Jack replied that he was not a Biblical scholar just a literary critic and historian. That was Jack's job. But he added "If anyone thinks the Gospels are either legends or novels, then that person is simply showing his incompetence as a literary critic."

In Jack's long literary career he had read a great deal of novels. He was a wide and varied reader and was what you call an expert on legends from ages past. Jack knew perfectly well that the Gospels were not that kind of stuff.

He announced emphatically that the gospels were 'absolutely full of the sort of things that don't come into legends.'

"The war, the whole of life, everything tended to seem pointless. We needed, many of us, a key to the meaning of the universe. Lewis provided just that," wrote Air Chief Marshal Sir Donald Hardman of Jack's radio broadcast. These broadcasts were given from 1941 to 1943 in London when it was under heavy German bombardment.

Jack was overwhelmed with letters from listeners. "I need some help Warnie! Could you give me a hand?" he asked his brother.

"Certainly, Jack. Just tell me how."

"Well, if I get a letter from a serious enquirer I will answer it in longhand!" said Jack. "You, Warnie, can type up the more or less standard letters."

The "serious enquirers" were huge in number

and probably the most sacrificial form of unselfishness in the life of C. S. Lewis was his letter writing. The more his fame grew the more people wrote to him to argue, seek help, express appreciation or to build friendship. They were all answered. Even when his hand grew rheumatic he doggedly kept going. In fact his collected letters to one woman were eventually published as a book called *Letters to an American Lady*. People greatly treasured a letter from C. S. Lewis, including children.

Jack's talks on radio were all eventually published together in a single volume entitled *Mere Christianity* and although many millions enjoyed these talks, he did have his critics. Alistair Cook, the famous broadcaster, considered Jack's view of sex and marriage "puritanical" and powerful logic as "pat oversimplification".

"A pious paradox-monger and audacious word-juggler," wrote Victor Yarros in *American Freeman*. Jack was undeterred. He kept going for God.

"Could you possibly talk to men in the Royal Air Force, Mr. Lewis," asked the Rev. Maurice Edwards who was the Chaplain-in-Chief of the R.A.F. in the winter of 1941.

"I doubt my ability to talk to service men," said Jack, "But I am willing to try."

He tried. From the mountainous areas of Scotland and central Wales as well as across England, all through his summer holidays every weekend was spent at R.A.F. camps speaking to men about the Christian faith.

Many were encouraged and strengthened by what Jack had to say to those service men and women. Many men who had never bothered about church before heard, for the first time, about the Lord and Saviour Jesus Christ. C. S. Lewis was very concerned for young pilots who were going out on bombing missions and facing death almost every night of their lives. He was very concerned for their souls and that they would come to a knowledge of the Lord Jesus as their Saviour. It was all busy, exhausting work but Jack gave himself to it wholeheartedly as he did to all his work.

"All atheists, agnostics, and those disillusioned about religion, or think they are," said the notice, announcing a meeting in the Junior Common Room at Somerville College, Oxford. What was it all about?

"There isn't anyone with whom to discuss our difficulties and doubts about the Christian faith," complained a student at the College.

"Well, let's do something about it," answered Stella Aldwinkle, the spiritual counsellor at the College. "I'll put up a notice announcing a meeting." It turned out to be quite a time.

"Churches are out of touch," said one student. "They don't ask the questions we are asking."

"That's because they can't answer them!"

answered another sceptic.

"Their services aren't relevant enough," complained another.

"Religious societies are no better," chipped in a disillusioned student. "There is no room for really open discussions about the difficulties with religion. It's just Christians who do the talking."

"We need a society which will be a meeting for open discussions where both believers and unbelievers can put their case."

"Done," said Stella Aldwinkle. "We will establish it under the name of The Oxford Socratic Club."

It was not long before Stella knew where she must go. She approached C. S. Lewis to see if he would be interested in such a Club.

"The Club is long overdue," said Jack.

"Well, will you do us the great honour of being our President, Mr. Lewis?" said Stella.

"Certainly, Miss Aldwinkle," said Jack.

So the Oxford Socratic Club began to meet on Monday evenings from January 1942. It very soon became the second largest Society in the whole University. The huge meeting began with a paper, that is, an article or essay read by either a Christian or an unbeliever. A speaker who held the opposing view would reply.

"The meeting is now open for discussion," the Chairman would declare. Everybody waited for that booming Irish voice. Jack often began by an attack on the unbeliever's position with his wit, wisdom and devastating logic. Some of the best known speakers in the nation spoke while Jack was President. Some students reckoned Monday evenings were the highest points of their university lives.

"What would you say Mr. Lewis attacked most?" people asked.

In fact the thing he attacked most was the point of view that morality, or people's views on right and wrong, are merely the result of people's personal feelings or prejudices. Some argued that a person's morality depended on his or her upbringing and what money they had or didn't have. C.S. Lewis did not agree with that. He also attacked the view that Christianity was a code of behaviour.

In the midst of all this hectic activity speaking, broadcasting, writing, lecturing, tutoring, administrating and preaching, C. S. Lewis still had to look after things at 'The Kilns', and Mrs. Moore, whose health was declining and who was beginning to be very, very difficult.

"Mrs. Moore was one of those who thrive on crisis and chaos: every day had to have some kind of domestic scene or upheaval, commonly involving the maids", wrote Warren, later. Poor Jack bore the brunt of this strife and upheaval. What made things even more difficult was the fact that the two maids who worked at 'The Kilns' constantly squabbled with each other. Then they would quarrel with Mrs. Moore!

"Pray for me," wrote Jack to a friend of his, "and for poor Mrs. Moore. There is never any time when all three women are in a good temper." Jack would pray to God about his problems and as a result would receive peace in his heart. As Mrs. Moore's health deteriorated she kept calling for Jack many times a day. She suffered from varicose veins in her legs that made walking very difficult.

"He is as good as an extra maid," Mrs. Moore once commented. No "maid" better kept the peace at 'The Kilns', that's for sure.

The evacuated children were kept entertained by Jack and he also spent many hours teaching a mentally retarded boy how to read and write.

"I do not like Warren's drinking, Jack," Mrs. Moore often complained.

"Neither do I," Jack would often reply. "It worries me very much but Warren is an alcoholic and alcoholism is an illness. We must have pity upon him."

Poor Warnie was a "binge drinker", that is he went off into periods of very heavy drinking of alcohol after periods of moderation. It led to a lot of drunkenness which worried the life out of Jack, especially when Warren was away on Army duty and he could not get near to him. His drunken spells caused him to be put into hospital and that meant huge knock-on effects on the organisation of Jack's life. Warren paid the bills, answered the letters and organised Jack's schedules.

It is hard to credit that in the midst of all this

turmoil, pressure and responsibility Jack started to write the book which above all of his other books was to be the most loved. It was to be a book for children which would grip them as few other books have ever done. How could it be described? It is exciting, mysterious, entertaining, pleasing, deeply spiritual, shows infinite beauty and yet, all the time it flows naturally and easily into the mind. The book? It was about a Lion, a Witch and a Wardrobe.

"It was a Lion.
Huge, shaggy, and bright it stood facing
the risen sun.
Its mouth was wide open in song ... and
as he walked and sang the valley grew
green with grass."

C.S.Lewis
The character of Aslan,
from The Lion, The Witch
and The Wardrobe

Through the wardrobe

"What a fascinating old wardrobe, Mr. Lewis!" said one of the evacuated children staying at 'The Kilns', "Can I go inside and see if there's anything behind it?"

"By all means," said Jack.

"Now, there's a thought worth thinking about," Jack's mind reacted. "There might be a story there. I could explore the country that lies beyond the wardrobe!"

Did that child ever fully understand the amazing world she opened up? The question had been asked in September 1939 and it was not until Christmas 1948 that his famous book, *The Lion, The Witch and The Wardrobe* was largely finished. In the story Lewis made four evacuated children, Peter, Simon, Edmund and Lucy, go through a wardrobe into the land of Narnia which was in the grip of the White Witch. Edmund, unfortunately, is drawn on to the side of the White Witch and betrays the others. It takes the death of the Great Lion Aslan, the rightful ruler of Narnia, to bring about the redemption of Edmund. There then follows the mighty resurrection of Aslan, breaking the great Stone Table on which he had been slain.

The Lion, The Witch and The Wardrobe was to be the first of the seven Chronicles of Narnia. Since then the Lion, especially, has had an amazing effect on people, everywhere. Nowadays most people first encounter him on television productions or videos of the stories but he is an awesome character to come across as in *The Magician's Nephew* we read of him being present at the creation of Narnia:

"It was a Lion. Huge, shaggy, and bright it stood facing the risen sun. Its mouth was wide open in song ... and as he walked and sang the valley grew green with grass ... and every drop of blood tingled in the children's bodies, and the deepest wildest voice they had ever heard was saying: 'Narnia, Narnia, Narnia, awake. Love. Think. Speak.'"

Aslan, of course, was a symbol, a picture of Christ, the one to whom Jack had given his whole heart and life. How on earth did he ever create such wonderful stories? He explained the process in a lecture to the Library Association. He said, "I see pictures. Some... have a common flavour ... which groups them together. Keep quiet and watch and they will begin joining themselves up." Jack would sometimes be able to sit back and almost watch a story develop by itself. However, he admitted that this did not happen that often. More

often than not it involved a bit of hard work.
Stories didn't always come easy and Jack would
find himself having to fill in gaps with some
'invention'.

What kind of pictures did Jack have in mind
in 1948 when he wrote *The Lion, The Witch and
The Wardrobe*? Interestingly he had had a picture
in his mind since he was sixteen of a Faun carrying
parcels and an umbrella in a snowy forest! He had
other images in his mind throughout the years and
now he decided to tie them all together in a story.

"I had been having strange dreams about lions
when I began the work," Lewis wrote to little Ann
Jenkins, the ten year old child we were first
introduced to at the beginning of this story. One
thing is certain, the Lion then bounded into the
actual story and the rest is history!

There was, though, a huge hurdle to
overcome. It was the hurdle of his friend Professor
Tolkien. If anyone understood the whole process
of creating another world through writing, it was
J. R. R. Tolkien. In fact one thing that Jack Tolkien
agreed on was that any truly successful romantic
writing should give the reader an entry into
another world.

Back in the Hilary Term of 1933 Jack had
first read a manuscript Tolkien had given him. It
began with the words, "In a hole in the ground
there lived a hobbit ..." Tolkien had been telling his
four children bedtime stories about hobbits for
years and, encouraged by Jack and a few others,

he had expanded the stories, arranged them into chapters, and typed the handwritten script into typed script on his huge Hammond typewriter. Jack just loved the stories that emerged.

"That character Bilbo Baggins that you have created even looks and sounds like you, Tolkien!" Jack said.

"I freely admit it," the great writer replied. "I am not as well-to-do as Bilbo but I am middle-aged, do dress in sensible clothes but with a splash of colour in my waistcoat, I do like food unrefrigerated and I would, if given the field, pick my own mushrooms!"

Now, though, Jack faced a huge problem. The great Tolkien did not like his new work.

"I think the book is almost worthless," Tolkien said to Jack after he had finished reading him a story.

"Worthless?" thought Jack, "It's not worth publishing!"

"What's worthless about it?" he asked.

"Well, you have got all sorts of creatures in your imaginative country Narnia and they come from very different sources and I think it's hopeless to put them all together in the same country! It just won't work. I mean Fauns and a White Witch, Father Christmas and Nymphs, beavers and a lion; what a mixture! It's too much of a jumble."

"But all these kinds of characters can exist in our heads," said Jack with a pleading voice.

"Not in mine, or at least not at the same time," answered Tolkien.

Jack wondered what he should do. Should he publish the book?

"Of course you should publish the story," said his old pupil Rodger Lancely-Green, author of the story *The Wood That Time Forgot* and *King Arthur and his knights of the Round Table*. "I like the story. Though, I'm not sure about having Father Christmas in it."

"Come on, Mr. Lewis, it's a super story. I think children will fall in love with the book all over the world," said Mary Clare, the daughter of Jack's doctor, Humphrey Havard. She was right. In their millions children have responded showing that there is some world of imagination that we all share. Jack had struck spiritual gold and though Tolkein didn't gather it, others did. In fact, not only did they gather it, they delighted in it. With many children it does not seem to matter how many times the story is told to them they continue to relish and revel in it and when they grow up, say that it is by far their favourite children's book.

"I doubt if it will sell," said Geoffrey Bles, Jack's publisher, "People might not like it and it will affect the sales of your other books." Happily, Mr. Bles said that if the book had to be published then it should be the first of a series of children's stories.

By the end of 1948 Jack had written *Prince Caspian* and so one Narnia book was published every year until 1956. Geoffrey Bles soon found he had huge sales on his hands. In the books children became aware of the eternal world through the seemingly ordinary, and that is what Jack meant to convey. It was, of course, how Jesus told stories, too. Isn't it incredible how God uses people? As I talked recently to the Rt. Hon. David Bleakley, a friend of C. S. Lewis's, he commented that Jack "had no delusions of grandeur because he was so grand he didn't need to have!" I laughed. What David meant of course was that C. S. Lewis was grand in the proper Christian sense. He was unaware of his greatness, of the powerful way God was using him. He was losing his life for Christ's sake and finding it. That was his true greatness and grandeur!

David told me he used to walk with Jack to and from their work in Oxford nearly every day, as they only lived a stone's throw from each other. Jack would enter the door of 'The Kilns' and Mrs. Moore would say, "Boysie," her nick name for Jack, "get me a half a stone of potatoes."

"I'll have to go, David," he would say and climbing on to his bike he would go to the local shops, get the potatoes and bring them back on the handlebars of his bike! David still laughs at the number of things Jack could get on those handlebars.

"He would often get down on his knees and scrub the floor," David told me. What a story! The man who took us all through the wardrobe, who

showed us that this life is not all there is, was so
heavenly minded he was of great earthly use. He
became one of the greatest servants of God in this
century leading an untold number of children and
adults to the Christian faith.

Life was no paradise for him, though. He was
passed over for a Merton Professorship of Modern
English Literature. Why? It seems some electors
were against Jack because he had not produced
enough scholarly work! Popular religious books
did not weigh heavily with the electors. Overwork
and exhaustion brought on illness in the summer of
1949 and Jack found himself in the Acland Nursing
Home in Oxford. He had hoped for a holiday in
Northern Ireland but Warren fell into heavy
drinking again and Jack had to cancel his visit. His
busy life surged on with the increased burden of
Mrs. Moore's incapacity to get about.

"She must immediately go to a Nursing
Home," said the doctor.

"You mean, now?" asked Jack.

"Yes, this is the third time she has fallen out
of bed and we cannot risk another."

"I shall cancel a planned holiday
immediately," said Jack.

"I am in a whirl of relief, pity, hope, terror
and bewilderment. Pray for me," he wrote to his
friend, Arthur Greeves.

Poor Mrs. Moore had now lost her mind and
she constantly grumbled, blasphemed and shouted
out nasty things. Then she would burst out crying.

"Please, pray for her," said Jack to his friends.

"Good-day Mr. Lewis, back again to see Mrs. Moore? That's nearly every day now," said the nurse on seeing Jack at Mrs. Moore's bedside once more.

"She needs me," he replied. She died in January 1951 of influenza and although she does come in for a lot of criticism for being too demanding on Jack's time, making him do a lot of domestic chores, the truth is that we all owe her a lot in that she kept him down to earth and that made his writing all the more accessible to millions of people who have to lead very tedious and often boring lives.

It has been pointed out that Jack put Mrs. Moore into *The Lion, The Witch and The Wardrobe*. It is reckoned that Mrs. Beaver was Mrs. Moore's character at its best. With trout hissing in the pan; potatoes boiling in a pot; a jug of creamy milk for the children ... and in the middle of the table, "a great big lump of deep yellow butter". It had to be Mrs. Moore's table at 'The Kilns'. It was Mrs. Beaver who said that nothing could beat "Fresh water fish if you eat it when it has been alive half an hour ago and has come out of the pan half a minute ago". Except perhaps "a great and gloriously sticky marmalade roll, steaming hot", which had just come out of the oven. "And when each person has got his (or her) cup of tea, each person has shot back his (or her) stool so as to be able to lean against the wall and give a long sigh of contentment." Jack may not always have sighed with contentment with the sharp-tongued lady by the breakfast table but one thing is for certain: he had made a promise to Paddy Moore thirty-four years previously and God, and those who were near to him, knew how very well he had tried to keep it.

Sadly, Jack was also passed over for the position of Professor of Poetry at Oxford in 1951. It again seems that his constant preaching of the Christian Gospel annoyed many of the senior members who voted in the election. Jack's faith cost him a lot but he shrugged it off.

He did eventually get his holiday in Ireland in 1951, staying at the Crawfordsburn Inn near Bangor, County Down, and walking the scenes of his childhood.

"It's wonderful to be home again, Arthur," he said enthusiastically. "I need all this beautiful scenery and fresh air." He came back the following year to Southern Ireland and toured the island by car.

Jack must have looked a rare sight, stepping off a train or lecturing in the Great Hall at Oxford, with his old brown Harris tweed jacket, his well worn baggy brown corduroy trousers, his patterned well-washed shirt with an unremarkable tie. His face had a fresh healthy colour and his eyes sparkled with laughter. Sometimes when he went to lecture he would begin as soon as he entered the room, sometimes from the back, with his booming voice, talking all the way to the podium. Famous, gifted, godly and enormously kind, Jack still lacked one thing: the love of a woman for him.

Soon, though, despite the hectic pace at which he lived, love was going to cross his path and bring him such happiness as he had never known. Her name was Joy.

The Story-teller

"Wilt thou love her, comfort her, honour
and keep her
in sickness and in health:
and forsaking all others,
keep thee only unto her
so long as ye both shall live?"

The Form of Solemnization of Matrimony

Surprised by joy

There is no musical that describes the life of a
Jewish community in a village setting better than
Fiddler On The Roof. Set in Eastern Europe it
shows the effect of Jewish laws and rituals upon a
family. The role of the little "Nosey Parker" in a
village community, poking her nose in and out of
people's lives, has been pricelessly caught in the
famous song, *Matchmaker, matchmaker, make me
a match*.

In 1940 a novel called *Anya* was published. It
gives a wonderfully rich account of Jewish village
life in the Ukraine before the first World War. The
writer was called Joy Davidman and her parents
were Jews from Europe and the novel could have
come right out of a scene in *Fiddler On The Roof*.
They had emigrated to New York City and their
daughter Joy, on graduating in English Literature
at Columbia University, became an English teacher
in various New York high schools.

Joy was an atheist and became poetry editor
of a Communist paper called, *New Masses*. She

also worked for a time as a Hollywood script writer and had married another Communist called Bill Gresham. They had two children, David and Douglas. Eventually Bill and Joy left the Communist Party being very disillusioned with its ideas.

"Bill, you must really stop drinking all that alcohol," Joy constantly warned her husband, "You have so many gifts and talents but that stuff will kill you."

"I know. I know," Bill admitted.

"You are also far too extravagant with money and we will soon not have a roof over our heads," Joy also warned.

"What do you think I should do?" he asked.

"I think you should buy a farm, Bill," she answered. "That would give us a secure base as a family. You've made quite a bit of money from that film of your thriller, *Nightmare Alley*. Buy a farm with the proceeds from your film."

Bill agreed and Joy ran the farm while he continued to work as a magazine editor in New York City. One day the phone went at the farm. Joy answered.

"I'm going mad, Joy," said Bill's voice. "I don't know what to do. I can't bear to stay in the office and I cannot come home." He then put the phone down.

Joy was frantic. She tried to locate him with no success. Utterly helpless she later described how suddenly she felt God in the room with her.

Yes, she had long hidden from God and declared herself an atheist. Now God, in a deep personal way, had come near to her, and she sank to her knees and prayed. Joy's husband was moved by what Joy told him of God and he began to pray that God would help him overcome alcoholism. They began to attend church, regularly.

At this particular time the Gresham's had a friend called Chad Walsh who was an Episcopalian minister. Chad published the very first book ever written on Jack entitled *C.S. Lewis; Apostle of the Skeptics*. Joy talked to Chad about the influence that C.S. Lewis had upon her thinking. She told Chad how she longed to get some answers from C.S. Lewis about some of the points he had raised in his writing.

"Why don't you write him then, Joy?" said Chad. So it was that in January 1950 a letter arrived at 'The Kilns' from Joy Davidman to C. S. Lewis.

"That is an amusing and well written letter!" said Warren after Jack had given it to him to read.

"It demands a thoughtful reply," said Jack. So, back and forward the letters started to flow from Joy to Jack.

"I'd love to meet her some time," said Jack.

Bitterly for Joy her marriage to Bill was falling apart. He was unfaithful to his marriage vows and got involved with other women in his life. He was also drinking heavily again. Joy desperately wanted to talk to C. S. Lewis about her marriage difficulties and a book that she was writing on the Ten Commandments.

"Come and stay with me," wrote Joy's pen pal in London, Phyllis Williams. "You'd enjoy England." Joy jumped at the opportunity and left Douglas and David in the care of a cousin, Renee Pearse. Then she set off for England. Joy wrote to Jack from London and asked him to lunch with her and Phyllis.

"Rather lunch with me at my rooms at Magdalen College," replied Jack.

It was quite a meeting. Jack was intrigued at how straightforward Joy was in her views.

"I hate skyscrapers," she declared.

"You do?" said Jack.

"Inhuman things they are," she said. "People need to get out into the country and experience the fresh air and see nature uncrushed by the urban sprawl. Those skyscrapers are soul-less."

Jack, who of course, loved walking in the country, was with her all the way.

"I don't like modern America at all," Joy rattled on.

"Why not?" asked Jack.

"Oh! There's far too much new technology and advertisers could make anything sound exciting and sell it. It even affects literature. Those publicists make bad writing appear wonderful. It's dragging down literature, Mr. Lewis."

After eating, Jack showed Joy and Phyllis around the College. Joy was overwhelmed with excitement about it all, poking fun questions at Jack and showing a deep interest in the life and history of his College.

"Tell me Mrs. Gresham, about your education," said Jack as he led the way around Magdalen College.

"I learned to read before I was three," she replied. "I entered Hunter College in New York City at the age of fifteen and graduated at the age of nineteen. I acquired a Masters Degree in English from Columbia University at the age of twenty-one."

"You must meet my brother Warren," said Jack, "If you would return to lunch here at Magdalen."

"I'd be delighted," replied Joy.

"I'll invite you again soon," said Jack.

He did just that. On arrival he introduced her to Warren and several other guests.

"Mrs. Gresham has spent some time in Hollywood," said Jack as they sat down.

Joy was coaxed into telling Jack and Warren about her experiences of Hollywood.

"The film company Metro-Goldwyn Meyer always sent out scouts every now and again to Eastern Colleges in the United States to look out for promising young script-writers," she said. "Your University had already published my poems entitled, *Letter to a Comrade* and the publishing company Macmillan had accepted my novel, *Anya* so I was picked".

"How did you get on in Hollywood?" asked Jack, intrigued.

"Oh, I wrote four screen plays but M.G.M. didn't like them," answered Joy. "After six months in Hollywood I returned to New York."

"What year was that Mrs. Gresham?" asked Warren.

"1939," she replied.

"I missed you by nine years," said Warren, telling of his own tour of Los Angeles and the set of *The Taming of The Shrew* produced in 1929 starring Douglas Fairbanks and Mary Pickford.

"The houses were enormous, the lawns were massive, the swimming pools superb," expanded Warren.

"Is there anywhere in this monastic establishment," interrupted Joy, "where a lady can relieve herself?" She was quickly shown the nearest loo!

Knowing that Joy Gresham had to sail for New York on 3rd January Jack and Warren invited her to spend Christmas 1952 with them at 'The Kilns'. Joy prepared a wonderful Christmas dinner and an enormous turkey with all the trimmings.

"You don't mind coming with me on long walks, Joy?" asked Jack. "I really do love walking."

"Not at all," she replied. "I just love it. It gets the head cleared and it is such a great opportunity to discuss ideas and even my new book, *Smoke on the Mountain*."

"There's a letter for you, Joy," said Jack one morning.

"Jack!" called Joy, shocked by what she read. "This is awful. Bill wants a divorce."

Joy returned to the United States and agreed to divorce Bill for even while she had been in Oxford, Bill had been unfaithful to her. She later returned to London and sent Douglas and David to a preparatory school in Surrey. Jack later paid for their expenses and even had them to stay for a holiday at 'The Kilns'.

"I'll take you up Magdalen Tower, boys," announced Jack, "There's a super view of Oxford from the top." They eagerly scrambled up the tower and had a look around. No sooner had they got to the ground than they eagerly looked at Mr. Lewis and said:

"Please can we do it again?"

"You fellows would certainly exhaust a fellow," said Jack. David and Douglas thought nothing of a four mile hike across the countryside on any given day!

"But it's such fun, Mr. Lewis, isn't it?"

"I have something to show you, boys," said Jack during the boys' holidays with their mother at 'The Kilns'. He brought out a typed copy of one of his new books called, *The Horse and His Boy*.

"I am going to dedicate this book to you both," said Jack.

The young boys did not realise it at the time but Jack was paying them one of the greatest compliments that could ever be paid and to this day whenever *The Horse and The Boy* is read, the Gresham boys are remembered.

In 1954 a great change came into Jack's life. He became very concerned that the study of Old English was becoming unpopular with younger members of the Oxford teaching staff. This was a subject which was very close to Jack's heart and he spoke out about it.

"Let's do something about Jack" his friends and admirers said. "Let's create a special position for him in Cambridge so he can immerse himself in the teaching and promotion of Old English".

Jack was flabbergasted. "I am overwhelmed," he said on being offered the position of the Professorship of Medieval and Renaissance Studies. Jack could now encourage the study of the literature of the Middle Ages and of the great revival of learning in the fourteenth to sixteenth centuries called The Renaissance.

"Will we buy a house in Cambridge, Warnie?" asked Jack.

"It means selling this one," said Warnie, "and we can't do that, Jack, because Mrs. Moore only left us this house until our death. I really need to stay here to do my work on the seventeenth-century in France." Warnie was quite a scholar on this part of French history and his work on it was published.

"I must admit, Warnie, I truly love Oxford as a place to live," said Jack.

"A compromise is called for," said Jack's friends on hearing of his dilemma. "Why not live here from Monday to Friday and go back to Oxford for the weekends and Monday mornings?"

"Agreed," said Jack in reply. "It's the best of both worlds."

"What's this chap Lewis like?" said a student to his friend, a former pupil of Jack's, as they joined the huge crowds on their way to Jack's opening, or inaugural lecture at Cambridge.

"Extraordinary," said the former pupil, "There's no-one quite like him."

"Look at this crowd," said another, who couldn't find a seat in the crowded lecture hall and had to mount the platform behind Jack to find one, "What's he got?"

"The great ability to say complicated things simply," said his neighbour, waiting with eagerness to hear what Jack had to say. It was a superb lecture, full of wit and life and verve and power.

Jack made a plea for the importance of the English writers of the medieval and renaissance period and referred to himself as an old "Western man". He also called himself, in literature terms, "A dinosaur!" The crowd gave him a huge and enthusiastic round of applause.

Joy helped Jack to move to Cambridge which he found friendlier than Oxford. She helped him with more than the move.

"I've run out of ideas for writing, Joy," Jack declared one day.

"What? Jack, I can't believe it!"

"It's true," said Jack depressingly. "No pictures come into my mind any more."

"Then I'll help you," said Joy.

They sat down in comfortable chairs and began to discuss ideas together. When one surfaced, Jack went to work.

"I've written the first chapter," said Jack the following evening.

"Let me see it," said Joy immediately, carefully reading what he had written and then criticising it. Soon the next chapter was written and in a month it was almost completed. The book was called, *Till We Have Faces*, and is judged to be one of his most important works.

In 1954 Bill Gresham divorced Joy and in 1955 she moved with her boys to a house in Oxford, leased for her by Jack. Jack also paid for the rent. She continued to help him with his writing.

One day in April 1956 Jack called in at the leased house at No. 10 Old High Street, Oxford to find Joy in a real dilemma.

"What's up, Joy?" he enquired.

"The British Home Office will not renew permission for me as an American citizen to live and work in the United Kingdom," she said.

"Why ever not?" said Jack, greatly surprised. "Did they give any reason for their refusal?"

"No reason whatsoever," replied Joy raising her hands with exasperation. "Though, mind you, I think it is probably because I was once a member of the Communist Party. Truth is, Jack, I wasn't a quiet member either, I took a very public stand for Communism before I was disappointed and disillusioned with the whole thing."

"Do you think you could go back to the United States, Joy?" asked Jack.

"No, I couldn't go back. For a start Bill would try to persuade Douglas and David to stay with him and leave me. Then I would have to constantly listen to my parents going on about the awful mess I had made of my life. Anyway, I have said goodbye to the United States in my book, *Smoke On The Mountain*. I desperately want to stay in England, Jack, and the only way I can think of doing that is to become a British citizen. The problem with that is that if the British are kicking me out because I was once a Communist there is not much chance that they would allow me to become one of them, is there?"

"Well," said Jack in one of the most important replies he ever made in his life. "If you have only got to the end of April then the only way you can become a British citizen is to marry a British citizen!"

"Are you proposing to me, Jack?" said Joy with an impish smile.

"No, no, no!" replied Jack swiftly. "I am far too old to propose. Anyway, if you were ever to get married again, Joy, you should marry a younger man than me. What I have in mind is a proposition."

"What kind of proposition, Jack?" said an intrigued Joy.

"I propose that you and I go to the Register Office here in Oxford and we get married in a civil ceremony as opposed to a church ceremony. No-one would really know about it but the British Home Office. Owen Barfield could draw up a paper we could both sign that would say the marriage was nothing but a move to get around the problem of your being refused permission to stay and work in Britain. You could have the marriage made invalid whenever you want. We could continue to live in separate houses."

"But Jack, wouldn't such a marriage compel you by law to financially support me and my boys?" said an amazed Joy.

"Oh! I have done that anyway for some time, Joy, and I would be glad to continue to do it."

On Monday, 23rd April, 1956 Joy Gresham limped into the Register Office at 13 St. Gile's, Oxford. The doctor reckoned she was suffering from fibrositis. Jack arrived and in the presence of two friends stood before the Superintendent Registrar, Cecil W. Clifton and went through a civil marriage ceremony with Joy Gresham.

Strange as it may seem Jack was positively not, at this time, actually in love with Joy. We know this because Jack told his friend George Sayer that this was a fact. He had gone through with a civil ceremony of marriage with Joy just to allow her to stay in the country with her boys.

He liked her, appreciated her gifts and laid great importance to her opinions. She was his friend but that was as far as it went. Even some of his best friends did not immediately know of his marriage. He continued to be very kind to the Gresham boys.

"Brilliant," said Douglas. "It's so kind of you. I've always wanted a horse."

Jack bought the horse and had it stabled at 'The Kilns'. The boys spent their holidays there.

Slowly, though, Joy began to complain of pain she was experiencing.

"I have got pains in my leg, my back and my chest," she kept saying.

Joy's doctor had diagnosed her condition as fibrositis which is inflammation of the lesions of the muscle sheaths. She had accepted this diagnosis and went on with her work.

One October evening in 1956 Joy found herself in such pain, round about eleven o'clock she wondered whether or not she should phone Jack in Cambridge. Suddenly she tripped on the telephone cord and as she tried to keep her balance, she heard something snap. It was as though she had stepped on a twig. She fell to the floor with a scream.

"Help! Help!" she cried, managing to attract the attention of a neighbour who ran to her aid.

"Are you all right? Are you all right?" said a voice in her ear. It was her friend Katherine Farrer who had suddenly felt something was wrong with

Joy and had called to see her at just the right moment.

Joy was taken immediately by ambulance to the Wingfield Morris Orthopaedic Hospital which was about a quarter of a mile from Joy's home. When X-rays were taken it was revealed that her left thigh-bone had been broken and that cancer was the cause.

Jack arrived the next day from Cambridge having heard by telephone just that morning of Joy's being rushed to hospital. She told him the sickening facts.

"I am sorry I am such a burden," she said, wearily. "How are you going to pay for this, Jack? The hospital thinking I am an American citizen will bill me but if they knew I was Mrs. C. S. Lewis, British citizen, then I will get the treatment free!"

"I'll worry about that when the time comes," said Jack. At that moment a nurse arrived to give Joy more medication. Jack rose to leave.

"Would you like something to read?" he asked.

"How about your book, *The Problem of Pain*, that would be nice," said Joy with a smile, teasing him.

"There is one chance in a hundred that she will be cured," Jack wrote to his friend Arthur Greeves in Northern Ireland in November 1956. "Fifty chances in a hundred that she will live as long as a year, seventy-five chances in a hundred that she will die in a few months."

"If this cancer doesn't kill me, this radiation treatment will! I am in absolute agony," said Joy as Jack sat by her bedside on Christmas Eve.

Jack quietly pulled a handful of letters from his pocket and gave them to her.

"Ah, this one is from my brother Howard," said Joy. "It is very friendly."

Jack sat quietly as Joy continued to read her letters. Another was from her parents asking what they could send to help her and a further came from relatives in Ireland offering to take her boys for the holidays.

"What on earth are you doing with a newspaper?" asked Joy, all of a sudden.

Jack spread a copy of *The Times* on her bed and turned the pages over until he came to Page eight. He then pointed to some small type.

"A marriage has taken place," she read, "Between Professor C. S. Lewis of Magdalen College, Cambridge, and Mrs. Joy Gresham, now a patient in the Churchill Hospital, Oxford."

"It is requested that no letters be sent," read Jack, aloud. Immediately Joy squeezed his hand!

By March 1957 the doctors had given up on Joy. They believed that her death was imminent. On March 20th Jack saw his former pupil, the Rev. Peter Bide at the hospital. Peter had once told Jack the story of how he was miraculously healed as a child. Jack had written to him and asked if he would come and pray for Joy's recovery by what was termed the "laying on of hands". This meant that the minister would place his hands on Joy as he prayed for healing.

"Would you do it now, Peter?" Jack pleaded.

"Are you looking for a miracle, Jack?" asked the minister.

"I am" he replied, quietly.

"Remember Jack, what happened once may not happen again" warned the minister as they moved towards Joy's hospital room.

After being introduced to Joy, the Rev. Bide gently laid hands on the dying woman and prayed for her healing. The very next day the Rev. Bide was back at Joy's bedside for what must have been one of the most moving moments in his life. It was 11 a.m. and Jack was holding Joy's hand as she lay in bed. Warren stood on one side of the bed and a nurse stood on the other. The Church of England minister read from *The Form of Solemnization of Matrimony*. He was, in fact, presiding over one of the most amazing religious ceremonies of the twentieth-century as he joined Joy Gresham in "holy matrimony" to the greatest Christian writer of the century. Jack and Joy had had a civil ceremony of a marriage of convenience but now Jack, who had fallen deeply in love with Joy, wanted with her to have a marriage ceremony solemnized in the presence of God.

"Wilt thou love her, comfort her, honour and keep her in sickness and in health: and forsaking all others, keep thee only unto her so long as ye both shall live?" asked the minister.

"I will", said Jack, fully expecting Joy to die very soon.

As soon as the ceremony was over Jack bent down to kiss his bride.

"Jack," she said immediately. "Now that the hospital can do no more for me and now that we have received the sacrament of matrimony, could I please have the consolation of dying at 'The Kilns' as Mrs. C. S. Lewis?"

"Of course, Joy," Jack replied, sadly.

"I may soon be in rapid succession a bridegroom and a widower." Jack wrote in a letter "There may in fact be a deathbed marriage."

"There seems little left to hope but that there may be no pain at the end," wrote Warren in his diary. Amazingly, in answer to prayer, incredible happiness was on the way.

'Christians never say goodbye!'
C.S. Lewis

On to beauty

At the beginning of April 1957 Joy returned to 'The Kilns' by ambulance. Death stared her in the face but Jack and Warren did their very best to make her comfortable. A nurse stayed with her full time, living in one of the guest rooms.

As Joy lay in the hospital bed which had been set up in the Common Room on the first floor, there seemed to be little to lift her spirits. Straps hung down in order that she might pull herself up but she didn't even have the strength to do that.

To add to Joy's troubles a letter arrived from the United States from her former husband, Bill Gresham. On hearing the news that Joy was about to die he wrote, referring to her sons Douglas and David, "Naturally, I shall want them to be with me in the event of your death."

He added that if this did not happen he would take them by force. The letter added greatly to Joy's distress and Douglas, on hearing the contents of the letter, wept. Immediately Jack rose to protect the boys and to relieve the distress of his

wife. He wrote two very strong letters to Bill
Gresham on the same day telling him that he had
"tortured one who was already on the rack" and
that there was nothing Joy dreaded as much as a
return of the boys to the charge of their father. He
pointed out that David and Douglas remembered
their father "as a man who fired rifles through
ceilings to relieve his temper, broke up chairs,
wept in public and broke a bottle over Douglas'
head." He stated that it was Joy's wish to have the
boys complete their education in England and to
enjoy the security of living at 'The Kilns'. He
warned Bill Gresham that if he tried to take the
boys against their will then he would have to face a
long and costly legal action against him.

Fortunately Bill Gresham decided to take a
less severe line. He realised that what Jack was
saying was true and that the boys were miserable
at the thought of returning to their father in the
United States. Joy and Bill continued to write
letters to each other to the end of Joy's life and
their content was, by and large, friendly. He never
again tried to persuade his boys to return to join
him in America.

Slowly, as spring gave way to summer, Joy
began to move about the house. Jack believed this
to be a very real answer to prayer. Strangely,
though, it was Jack who was now suffering pains.
He was suffering from a disease called
osteoporosis which caused his bones to weaken by
a fall in their calcium content.

"I'm losing calcium in my bones while you are gaining calcium in yours, Joy!" said Jack, "Isn't it a strange thing?"

It was actually true because within months Joy was walking again and the diseased spots in the bone were not spreading as before but disappearing.

"I'm afraid I shall have to fit you with a surgical brace to protect your spine, Jack," said his doctor.

"Why?" asked Jack.

"Because your osteoporosis has weakened you spine and it could break."

It was Jack who could hardly walk now. Throughout the summer he suffered a lot of pain but by the autumn his health began to improve with the help of steroids. He and Joy now entered what was, for them, the happiest period of their lives. They were both deeply in love.

"I'm going to improve the gardening on our estate, Paxford," Joy declared, one day, to the gardener.

"In what way, Mrs. Lewis?" said a surprised Paxford.

"Raise plants, please, in the greenhouse for flower gardening. Dig borders around the home, weed them and prepare them for planting flowers."

"I am not so keen on flower gardening, myself," said Paxford.

"Come on, Paxford, I am!" replied Joy.

"Let's improve this house, too, Jack," said

Joy, now full of new life. "We've got to make that old boiler of ours work, for once, and let's get the radiators re-connected."

"Great!" said Jack, "Why, I can now even have a hot bath!"

'The Kilns' was in fact often quite cold and had for years been heated with paraffin stoves.

"I am going to cook some evening meals, if that's OK, Mrs. Miller," said Joy to the cook.

"Wonderful, if you feel well enough to do it, Mrs. Lewis," replied Mrs. Miller.

"I'm going to draw a lot from your vegetable garden, Paxford," said Joy, "Jack needs healthy eating."

The house started to be full of activity.

"Let's redecorate this house, Jack, Let's do it inside and out," said Joy.

"Why, you are a busy bee, Mrs. Lewis," said Jack.

"I feel wonderful!" she said.

Did Jack believe in miracles? He certainly did. One day he was relaxing after dinner at Wescott House, which is a Church of England College at Cambridge University, when he picked up a book entitled *Windsor's Sermons* by the Rev. Alexander Didler. Waiting for his host to return he started to read the sermon entitled, *The Sign at Cana* which was a commentary of Jesus changing water into wine. After some time Jack's host, the Rev. Kenneth Carey, who was the Principal of Wescott College, returned.

"What do you think of the book, Jack?" asked the Rev. Carey.

"Isn't it incredible that we have had to wait nearly two thousand years before a theologian tells us that what the Church has always regarded as miraculous was in fact a parable?" said Jack with irony. He, of course, strongly disagreed with what the book was saying. The book was in fact trying to do away with the miraculous in the story.

"But that is the way much of the teaching about the New Testament is in these days," said the Rev. Carey.

"Are they denying what the Gospels say actually took place?" asked Jack.

"Well, they are denying some things but not others, Jack," the minister replied. "For example, they are not denying the resurrection."

"Ah!" replied Jack. "If they can swallow a camel like the resurrection why are they gagging on such gnats as the feeding of the multitudes?"

By this Jack meant, of course, that if people were prepared to believe that God could bring about the miracle of raising Christ's body from the dead, why could they not believe that he could bring about a much smaller miracle like feeding the five thousand with five barley loaves and two fish? Jack believed that a Church that abandoned the miraculous would be devastating and could have no real message of hope for the world.

"Do you believe in miracles?" he once asked his Ulster friend, David Bleakley.

"I do Jack," he replied.

"You'd have to be a realist to do so," said Jack.

So it was that Jack firmly believed that God had miraculously brought healing to Joy in answer to prayer. As a Christian he always taught the truth of the God of miracles.

"I would dearly love to show you my homeland, Joy," said Jack.

"I'd love to see Ireland," said Joy, "but let's ask the doctor what he thinks."

"I want to take Joy to Ireland on holiday this summer," said Jack to his doctor, "and I would like to go by sea, if possible, as I have always done."

"I advise against it," said the doctor. "If the sea were rough either of you might fall and that would be an absolute calamity in your condition. I advise you to go by air, Jack."

"But I am terrified of flying," answered the man who had created the story of Jill sent by Aslan to find the lost Prince Rilian on a night flight on the back of a great owl.

"You'd be OK," said the doctor.

"I don't know about that," said Jack. "It is the taking off that terrifies me."

Eventually the holiday was arranged and the Lewis's boarded their plane. All the way down the runway Jack prayed hard! He grasped the arm rests, his knuckles turning white. He was convinced the aircraft was out of control and was heading for a spectacular crash.

As the plane soared above the clouds and the vibrations lessened he and Joy peered out of the windows at the Welsh mountains far below and eventually the coastline of Northern Ireland with its headlands jutting out into the Irish Sea, as Jack put it, "brilliantly sunlit and standing out like a bit of enamel".

They were met at the airport by Arthur Grieves and driven to The Inn at Crawfordsburn. They stayed there for a few days, exploring County Down in Arthur's car. Then they went to Donegal where the weather was perfect. Jack could not credit the happiness that he had been allowed.

As summer turned to autumn and autumn to winter the quality of life continued to improve at 'The Kilns'. Towards Christmas a rather amusing incident arose. One day Warren had been travelling on a bus and had been sitting quite near an old woman. As the bus passed a church the old lady saw that a nativity crib had been placed at the front of the building.

"They bring religion into everything," she muttered. "Look - they're dragging it into Christmas now!"

When Warren told Jack the story he laughed heartily and put the story into his many Christmas letters. In Narnia, of course, it was always winter and never Christmas but in Jack's home Christmas was very important indeed. The story of the old lady emphasised how far people can get from the real meaning of what Christmas is all about. Jack's heart and pen were one hundred percent at the service of the Saviour born at Bethlehem, who is Christ the Lord. Any Christmas card that he sent out that year had on its front an engine with a string of carriages chugging merrily towards some hills. On the back the train was identified as the Talyllyn Railway which ran a narrow-gauge train in Wales, any profits from the sales of the cards would go to the preservation of the ninety-seven year old railway. The message read, "With best wishes for a merry Christmas and a Happy New Year." It was proving to be a very happy Christmas for Jack and Joy for they had fully expected death to visit them. The New Year stretched out with much brighter prospects than they had dreamed.

Recently Jack had been thinking of writing about the subject of love. He mused on the fact that there were four words in Greek for love. There was the word "Storge" which means affection. We can have affection for a teddy bear or an old coat as much as for people. Then there is the word "Philia" which means friendship such as people can have for friends they go on holiday with or who share the same sport. The word "Eros" is love between the sexes but the word "Agape" is love in the Christian sense, which is love for the unlovable. This, of course, is the love God has for us. Jack's work on the subject was eventually published in his book, *The Four Loves*. He had now certainly experienced all four loves

himself. "Eros," though, was to be overwhelmed
once more with grief and depression. In the
summer of 1959 Joy's cancer returned and with it,
the pain. The effects of the therapy that Joy
received and the pain she experienced did not
diminish her sense of humour and fun.

"We've just been to Greece," said Rodger and
June Lancelyn-Green on returning from a holiday
in April 1959. They were good friends of Jack and
Joy and enthused about the breathtaking country
of Greece. "What an incredible place it is. The
ruins! The Parthenon! Athens! The Islands! The
sunshine! What a place!"

"I would have given anything to be with
you," said Joy.

"Why don't we all go together on a similar
tour next year? I'll arrange it all," said Rodger.

"What a good idea!" said Jack, who was
delighted to have the opportunity of travelling
somewhere Joy had wanted to visit all her life.

In the Easter holidays of 1960 Joy and Jack
flew to Athens and stayed in Greece for eleven
days. It is not hard to imagine how Jack's mind in
particular was stimulated by the land of myths and
legends. They climbed the Acropolis, visited
Mycenae and the Gulf of Corinth, they went to
Attica, Delphi and Rhodes. They spent three days
in Heraklion, the capital of Crete and thoroughly
enjoyed excursions through the Cretan
countryside.

The creator of Narnia now visited the

restorations at Knossos on Crete and he who had studied ancient Greek and Roman Literature and culture for most of his life, simply exulted in the Mediterranean scenes where it all began. His wife, though, was dying, and he knew it. Every day with her was precious. Just a few weeks after their longed for holiday in Greece life took a sudden twist.

As it turned out the days that Joy and Jack had left together were not to be long. At a quarter past six on Wednesday morning, July 11th, 1960 Warren Lewis was awakened by Joy screaming and he went down to her. The doctor was called and gave her an injection. At 1.30 p.m. she was taken into hospital by ambulance and died, peacefully, at 10.15 p.m. that same night. Later Jack wrote an epitaph which he stated that he wanted to have on a stone plaque installed at the Headington Crematorium to commemorate his wife. The epitaph read:

> "Here the whole world, stars, water, air,
> And field and forest, as they were
> Reflected in a single mind
> Like cast-off clothes was left behind
> In ashes, yet with hope that she
> Reborn from wholly poverty,
> In lenten lands, hereafter may
> Resume them on her Easter Day."

After Joy died Jack found it very hard to pray.

The Story-teller

He constantly thought of Joy and their life together and he decided to write a book about how he felt. Because he knew so many people would write to him in huge numbers if he put his name to the book, he published under a pseudonym or fictitious name. He called himself N. W. Clerk. Eventually, though, the book was republished in his own name in 1964. The book is entitled, *A Grief Observed*, and untold numbers of people have been touched and helped by it, especially those who have just been bereaved. It is, of course, a very sad book, as this extract shows:

"I have no photograph of her that's any good. I cannot even see her face distinctly in my imagination ... but her voice is still vivid. The remembered voice - that can turn me at any moment to a whimpering child ... Did you ever know, dear, how much you took away with you when you left?" But the triumph of the Christian faith comes through, powerfully when he writes "She is in God's hand. That gains a new energy when I think of her as a sword ... now perhaps He ... makes lightenings with it in the air. 'A right Jerusalem blade'."

The number of letters Jack received was now greater than he had ever known. The enormous interest his book stirred in people's hearts, the chords of sympathy he struck, the help and inspiration his writing gave to children, to teenagers, to adults was incalculable. He had no idea that he was to become the best selling

Christian author of all time. But those letters kept pouring in to 'The Kilns' and Jack now spent much time during his weekends answering them.

He continued writing and also meeting his friends every Monday morning at "The Lamb and Flag" or "Eagle and Child". He also continued working from Monday to Friday at Cambridge.

Unfortunately, his kidneys got infected and around June 1961 he began to feel unwell. He then suffered from blood poisoning and as his condition worsened he had to have blood transfusions. He was not fit enough for an operation.

"I am afraid, Professor Lewis, you had better not go to bed at night. It is better that you sleep upright in a chair," he was advised.

Throughout this time Jack kept very close to the Lord. God never left Jack - he stayed with him throughout it all.

Thankfully Jack never lost his sense of humour either. Throughout his troubles and subsequent illnesses he often remained cheerful and optimistic. On July 16th, after being admitted to the Acland Hospital Jack had a heart attack and became unconscious. The following afternoon at 2 p.m. the Curate of St. Mary Magdalene's, the Rev. Michael Watts gave Jack what is termed in the Church of England extreme unction. Jack was anointed with oil in a sacramental ceremony to prepare him for death. Suddenly at 3 p.m Jack awoke from his coma, took off his oxygen mask and said: "Can I have a cup of tea, please?"

A nurse immediately ran to a telephone and rang his friends, Walter Hooper and Austin and Katherine Farrer. They rushed to the hospital immediately.

"Is there anything wrong?" asked Jack.

"You have been asleep for quite a while," said Austin. "We were concerned about you."

Jack started to improve and one day a lady quietly tiptoed into his hospital room and took his hand.

"Jack, it's Maureen," she said. It was Maureen Moore for whom he had provided for so long. She had been warned that because of his condition he did not always recognise people.

"No," he replied smiling, with his eyes still closed, "it's Lady Dunbar of Hempriggs."

"Oh Jack," replied Maureen, "how could you remember that?"

"On the contrary, how could I ever forget a fairytale?" said Jack.

Amazingly, only recently, Maureen had succeeded to a Baronetcy in Scotland. She was now a titled lady and the owner of a castle and a huge estate. If Paddy, her brother, had lived he would have become a Baronet!

Jack still, unfortunately, craved cigarettes and didn't like the rule of the hospital matron.

"You are allowed to smoke, Professor Lewis, as long as there is someone else in the room," she said, "you are not allowed to have matches, otherwise you will light-up and with your medical condition you may fall asleep and the cigarette in your hand will set this hospital on fire!"

"Give me a box of matches that I can hide under my bedclothes!" Jack badgered his young American friend, Walter Hooper. Walter gave in and Jack immediately hid the matches.

When Walter left the room a nurse appeared.

"I just want to tidy up Professor Lewis," she said. As she fixed his bedclothes she discovered the matches.

"Got you!" she yelled with triumph and confiscated them immediately like a teacher with a disobedient pupil.

"How do they know?" asked Jack as soon as Walter returned, "That nurse found my matches and confiscated them!"

"Ah, sorry Jack," said a blushing Walter, "I told her about them!"

"I have what no friend ever had before," said Jack in his loud bullish voice but with a smile added, "I have my own private traitor! Can I have another box of matches?"

It was clear that Jack was going to need a nurse when he went back to 'The Kilns' after hospital. Walter was now engaged as Jack's secretary and would care for him during the day. But who would care for him at night? A male nurse called Alec Ross was recommended. He was a Scotsman.

It was not long before he had made his mark on the situation. His standard of hygiene was very high and soon the kitchen at 'The Kilns' shone like a hospital lab. Alec bedded down in the music room.

Almost the very first letter Jack worked on after his return to 'The Kilns' was a letter of resignation from his Professorship of Medieval and Renaissance Literature at Magdalene College at Cambridge. It must have been a difficult letter to write because Jack had a huge affection for his work at Cambridge. Walter had told Jack exactly what had happened to him, explaining that he had had a heart attack, had gone into a coma and had been expected to die. Jack thanked him for telling him the truth.

"I am now unofficially an extinct volcano," wrote Jack to a friend in August, his humour still bubbling to the surface despite his illness.

"Now Walter," said Jack towards the end of the month, "you and Douglas must go to Cambridge and bring me back my books."

"We'll hire a lorry," said Walter. They both set to work and organized transportation of up on two thousand books!

"Where are we going to store these?" said Walter on returning to 'The Kilns'. Most of the available space was already packed with books.

"Follow me!" said Jack, picking up a handful of books with a twinkle in his eye and heading for the music room. There lying fast asleep in a bed in the corner lay the nurse Alec Ross, snoring away. For the next hour or so the three men tip-toed into the room carrying books which they piled up the walls virtually to the ceiling. Suddenly Alec awoke and screaming tried to flail his way out of the forest of books that had suddenly grown around him. The rest of the men fell apart laughing as books fell all around the hapless nurse. He eventually joined in the laughter!

Jack's final days were sad but were still pitted with his irrepressible humour. He was suffering from uraemia and continued to constantly fall asleep but again and again his ability to look on the humorous side of life, surfaced.

One day the Farrers arrived for tea. Paxford, the gardener who did the shopping at 'The Kilns', always bought only half a pound of sugar at a time. Nobody could ever persuade him to buy more.

"Well," he would say, "you never know when the end of the world will come and we don't want to be left with sugar on our hands."

"Would it make any difference what was in the larder when the end comes?" joked Walter. "All I am asking is that Mr. Jack's guests enjoy their tea with sugar!"

"They might not take sugar," said Paxford.

"But they might," argued Hooper.

"But they might not!" replied Paxford, "And then where would we be?"

The Farrers arrived and a good time was had by all. As they departed, Jack and Walter stood at the door waving them off watching Austin, the tall and slim one and Katherine, the tiny one getting into their car. As they climbed in Jack, with a grin, turned to his friend Walter and quipped, "It was like entertaining elves!"

Throughout these days Jack kept up his reading and his mail still poured in, even more so since his illness had been announced in the newspapers. Walter Hooper helped him, daily, to deal with the deluge.

One recent letter was from an American University offering Jack £100 if he would speak via a telephone link-up to a classroom on any subject of his choosing for half an hour. He had written VPR at the top of the letter.

"What on earth does VPR stand for?" asked Walter.

"Very Polite Refusal," explained Jack.

"Why do you want to refuse?" asked Walter.

"Because I can write much better than I can speak," said Jack.

He may have amusingly referred to himself as an extinct volcano but the old volcano was still very capable of giving an eruption. Jack had been writing an article for a very famous American magazine called *The Saturday Evening Post*. When he received the proofs of the article to check them before publication he discovered that the last paragraph of his writing had been tampered with and changed. He was furious and immediately rang *The Saturday Evening Post* in New York.

"Publish the article as it was written or do not publish it at all!" he demanded.

It is interesting to note that Jack read a lot of his favourite books in his final days. They included the *Odyssey* and *Iliad* in Greek, *Aenid* in Latin, books by Dickens, Sir Walter Scott, Jane Austen's *Pride and Prejudice*, Fielding, Wordsworth's *The Prelude* and George Herbert.

Warren and Jack talked a lot now of their childhood and schooldays. As Warren put it, they went back to their "old schoolboy techniques of extracting the utmost from the last days of our holidays." Every night, though, Warren went to bed wondering if he were going to find Jack alive in the morning.

One fine autumn afternoon Jack's friend, George Sayer, head of English at Malvern College, got him in his car and drove him up Beacon Hill to the crest of the Chilterns and along the crest past Christmas Common. The beech trees were in their autumn glory. They stopped the car, opened the windows and gazed out at the incredible beauty around them. Jack was praying and praising God.

On Monday, November 18th, Jack was driven down to "The Lamb and Flag" for his last meeting of "The Inklings". On Wednesday, November 20th, he received Kaye Web of Puffin books, one of Jack's publishers, at 'The Kilns' and they talked of *The Chronicles of Narnia* and of some corrections that they felt were necessary. Yet when Kaye had gone, Jack had a rethink and turning to Warren he said words which, to all who love him and his works, bring great joy. They reveal that he was, in the end, a very fulfilled individual. "Behold the upright," wrote King David in Psalm 37: 37, "For the end of that man is peace." Was that true for Jack? It certainly was as he turned and said to his brother "I have done all that I was sent into the world to do. I am ready to go".

They are priceless words for a man who was about to die. He had two days left on this earth.

On Friday, November 22nd, 1963 Jack answered four letters in his own handwriting and fell asleep in his chair after lunch. Warren approached him and said, quietly:

"Jack, you might be more comfortable in your own bed."

"I agree, Warnie," he said.

About 4 p.m. Warren brought him a cup of afternoon tea, rousing him to take it. Jack was calm, and, as usual, cheerful, thanking his brother for the tea. He soon drowsed again.

At about 5.30 pm. Warren heard a crash in Jack's bedroom and running in found him lying unconscious at the foot of the bed. He shouted for help but before anyone could come, Jack had stopped breathing.

On the very same day as Jack died, President John F. Kennedy was assassinated in Dallas, Texas. Soon the whole world was filled with the tragic news and Jack's death was eclipsed by the American tragedy. Jack's funeral took place at Holy Trinity Church, Headington Quarry at 10 a.m. on Tuesday, November 26th, 1963. His death had been announced on the BBC news and an obituary appeared in *The Times*. Those at his funeral were mostly close personal friends.

A candle burned on top of Jack's coffin as it was carried to an open grave under a larch tree. We are told by one who saw it that its flame did not flicker. It was a beautiful symbol of all that Jack had been because he had shone as a light to millions across the world. Steadily and courageously he had "burned" as a Christian witness, especially to those who had little interest or enthusiasm for spiritual things and who saw themselves as atheists or agnostics.

"I believe in Christianity," he once wrote, "in the way I believe in the rising of the sun, not because I see it but because by it I see everything else." What he had seen he had, thankfully, shared.

What has happened in the years since the death of C. S. Lewis? The answer is that his legacy has grown stronger with every passing year. His enormous reputation rests on his writing. On this his centenary year, for example, three dozen of his books are still available with over forty million in print around the world. A play has been performed over the past years all over the world entitled *Shadowlands* about Joy and Jack's relationship and a major international film of the same name, starring Sir Anthony Hopkins and Deborah Winger, has been shown to millions.

The Chronicles of Narnia continue to be some of the favourite children's stories in the world. The BBC production of *The Chronicles of Narnia* has been hugely popular.

The Royal Shakespeare Company are playing *The Lion, The Witch and The Wardrobe* at Statford-on-Avon at the time of writing to rave reviews. Then there is *Jack*, a very moving and powerful musical portrait and celebration of the life and legacy of C. S. Lewis, written by Keith Getty and Douglas Gresham. This has recently been performed at Belfast City's prestigious "Waterfront Hall" close to Donegall Quay where Jack used to catch the ferry for Liverpool. Jack would not have believed all the fuss!

There has also been a Royal Mail C. S. Lewis stamp. Guided tours around the Northern Ireland Lewis trail have been held and a Lewis archive has been opened at the Public Records Office of Northern Ireland. The Rt. Hon. David Bleakley's book, *C. S. Lewis - At Home in Ireland* has just been published. Mary McAleese and Irish writers, Maeve Binchy and Seamus Heaney all express their appreciation of this great man.

There is a glowing tribute to C. S. Lewis from Dr. Billy Graham and from Christian leaders across Northern Ireland. Some of the most moving comments are by children from East Belfast where C. S. Lewis was born. They are hugely proud that this great story teller came from their city.

In the United States at the moment C. S. Lewis is arguably the most quoted Christian writer in the nation with millions of readers. An incredible number of people have come to put their trust in the Lord Jesus Christ as Saviour and Lord as a result of reading his books.

There is no question that the memory of C. S. Lewis and his work will have continuing and profound influence. He is one of Ulster's precious gifts, by the grace of God, to the new millennium. Because he dealt in his writings with things of eternal consequence, there is an eternal consequence to his writings.

We have travelled on a long journey through the life of C. S. Lewis since we began it at the beginning of this book by meeting the little girl, Ann Jenkins who wrote to him all those years ago. One thing is certain, his life has been used of God to make the way to believe in Jesus very clear for great numbers of adults and children. That belief leads to a life beyond death which is indescribable. C. S. Lewis sums it up in his last book in the Narnia series, *The Last Battle*:

"The things that began to happen after that were so great and beautiful that I cannot write them ... now at last they were beginning Chapter One of the Great Story which no-one on earth has read: goes on for ever: in which every chapter is better than the one before."

How shall I finish the story of such a wonderful life? I have thought deeply about it and have decided to tell one more story from the life of this great storyteller.

One sunny winter's day in Oxford, many

years ago, C. S. Lewis and his young friend
Sheldon Vanauken, who had become a Christian
while a student at the University, dined at the
Eastgate, Oxford. They talked, strangely enough,
about death and what it would be like to awaken
after death. They agreed that it would be a sort of
coming home.

"Keep in touch, Sheldon," said Jack to his
American friend. "At all events we'll certainly
meet again, here or there."

They finished their meal and came out on to
the very busy High Street and shook hands.

Jack smiled before adding "I shan't say
goodbye. We'll meet again."

He then crossed the road and Sheldon stood
and watched him. When he reached the pavement
on the other side he somehow knew that Sheldon
would still be standing there in front of the
Eastgate. He turned and raised that famous voice
of his above the roar of the traffic. Heads turned
and, Sheldon records, at least one car swerved.

"Besides," Jack bellowed with a huge grin,
"Christians NEVER say goodbye!"

So, in this book, dear Jack, neither do I.

BIBLIOGRAPHY

Material for this book is based on the texts of
C. S. Lewis's works. I have, in addition, received
great help from the following books:
Jack, a life of C. S. Lewis, by George Sayer,
(Hodder and Stoughton, 1997).
The Secret Country of C. S. Lewis, by Anne Arnott
(Hodder and Stoughton, 1974).
C. S. Lewis at home in Ireland, by the Rt. Hon.
David Bleakley (Standtown Press, 1998).
C. S. Lewis - The Authentic Voice, by William
Griffen published by Lion.
A Severe Mercy, Sheldon Vanauken (Hodder and
Stoughton, 1997).
All my road before, edited by Walter Hooper,
Harper Collins.

HIGHLY RECOMMENDED

Rumours from the Sculptor's Shop, C. S. Lewis
Index. Compiled and Edited by Janine Goffar
(Solway, 1997). This is without question one of
the most useful books that have ever appeared on
C. S. Lewis. It makes what the great story teller
said on dozens of subjects easy to look up.

Lentent lands by the stepson of C.S. Lewis, Douglas H. Gresham (Harper Collins) This is a deeply
personal account of life with C.S. Lewis and Joy
Gresham.

BOOKS BY C. S. LEWIS

C. S. Lewis wrote a lot of material and the following list only highlights some of his great works. Where appropriate the current British publisher and/or imprint appears in square brackets at the end of the publication for each book (Fount and Fontana are imprints of Harper Collins).

The Lion, The Witch, and the Wardrobe, London: Geoffrey Bles, 1950 [HarperCollins]

Prince Caspian: The Return to Narnia, London: Geoffrey Bles, 1951. [HarperCollins]

The Voyage of the Dawn Treader, London: Geoffrey Bles, 1952. [HarperCollins]

The Silver Chair, London: Geoffrey Bles, 1953. [HarperCollins]

The Horse and His Boy, London: Geoffrey Bles, 1954. [HarperCollins]

The Magician's Nephew, London: Bodley Head, 1955. [HarperCollins]

The Last Battle, London: Bodley Head, 1956. [HarperCollins]

Surprised by Joy: The Shape of My Early Life,
London: Geoffrey Bles, 1955. [Fount]

The Four Loaves, London: Geoffrey Bles, 1960.
[Fontana]

Out of the Silent Planet, London: John Lane,
1938. [Pan]

The Problem of Pain, London: Geoffrey Bles,
Centenary Press, 1940 [Fount]

The Screwtape Letters, London: Geoffrey Bles,
1942. Reprinted, with a new letter and an addi-
tional preface, as *The Screwtape Letters and
Screwtape Proposes a Toast,* London: Geoffrey
Bles, 1961. The letters were first published in *The
Guardian*, a Church of England weekly. [Fontana]

Broadcast Talks, London: Geoffrey Bles, 1942.
Two series of broadcast talks (*Right and Wrong:
A Clue to the Meaning of the Universe* and *What
Christians Believe*) given in 1941 and 1942,
printed with some alterations.

*The Hideous Strength: A Modern Fairy Tale for
Grown-Ups*. London: John Lane, 1945. Abridged
by the author as *The Tortured Planet* (New York:
Avon Books, 1946) and as *That Hideous Strength*
(London: Pan Books, 1955). [*In The Cosmic
Trilogy*, The Bodley Head/Pan]

The Great Divorce: A Dream, London: Geoffrey Bles, Centenary Press, 1945. [Fontana]

Miracles: A Preliminary Study, London: Geoffrey Bles, 1947. Reprint with new version of chapter 3. London: Collins-Fontana Books, 1960 [Fount]

Till We Have Faces: A Myth Retold, London: Geoffrey Bles, 1956; New York: Harcourt, Brace and World, 1956. [Fount]

Reflections on the Psalms, London: Geoffrey Bles, 1958 [Fontana]

[N. W. Clerk, pseud.]. *A Grief Observed*, London: Faber and Faber, 1961. Reprinted as by C. S. Lewis, London: Faber and Faber, 1964.

Letters to Malcolm: Chiefly on Prayer, London: Geoffrey Bles, 1964. A selection of these letters, entitled *Beyond the Bright Blur*, was published as a limited edition for C.S. Lewis's friends (New York: Harcourt, Brace and World, 1963). [Fontana]

Collected Poems. Edited by Walter Hooper. London: Geoffrey Bles. 1964. [Fount]

Screwtape Proposes a Toast and Other Pieces, London: Collins-Fontana Books, 1965. [Fount]

God in the Dock: Essays on Theology and Ethics,
Edited and with a preface by Walter Hooper.
Grand Rapids, Mich.: Eerdmans, 1970. A paper-
back edition of the theological section was pub-
lished as *God in the Dock: Essays on Theology*
(London: Collins-Fontana Books, 1979) and as
Undeceptions: Essays on Theology and Ethics,
(London: Geoffrey Bles, 1971). [Both Fount]

*Fern-Seed and Elephants and Other Essays on
Christianity*, Edited and with preface by Walter
Hooper. London: Collins-Fontana Books, 1975.

The Dark Tower and Other Stories, Edited and
with a preface by Walter Hooper. London:
Collins, 1977; New York: Harcourt Brace
Jovanovich, 1977. [Fount]

All My road Before Me: The Diary of C. S. Lewis,
1922-1927. Edited by Walter Hooper. London:
HarperCollins 1991.

*Reference to the Teaching of English in the Upper
Forms of Schools, Riddell Memorial Lectures,
Fifteenth Series,* London: Oxford University
Press, 1943. [Fount]

THE LETTERS OF

C. S. LEWIS

Letters of C. S. Lewis, edited with a memoir by W. H. Lewis. Revised and enlarged edition edited by Walter Hooper. [Fount]
Letters to Children. [Fount]
Letters C. S. Lewis/Don Giovanni Calabria, translated and edited by Martin Moynihan [HarperCollins]
They Stand Together; The Letters of C. S. Lewis to Arthur Greeves, [Harper Collins]

HELPFUL MATERIAL
ON C. S. LEWIS'S FAMILY

The Lewis Papers by Major W. H. Lewis. This is an eleven-volume collection of family papers which may be consulted in the Bodleian Library of Oxford University in microfiche form or at The Wade Centre, Wheaton College, Wheaton, Illinois, U.S.A. Some of these are published in the following publication.
Letters of C.S. Lewis; Memoirs of the Lewis Family 1850-1930. Harper Collins UK, British Commonwealth and Harcourt Brace, United States of America.

We take this opportunity to acknowledge the following publishers: Harper Collins U.K. for permisson to print the 'Dear Ann' letter in all English speaking countries excpet the U.S.A. Harcourt Brace & Co. U.S.A. for permission to print the 'Dear Ann' letter in the United States.

ACKNOWLEDGMENTS

Christian Focus Publications acknowledge the following publishers as copyright holders for various quotes used within this book. These quotes comply with the copyright principle of fair comment or fair usage.

Quotes from the following titles:
Published by HarperCollins UK

Mere Christianity
Surprised by Joy
The Magician's Nephew
The Lion, The Witch and The Wardrobe
The Silver Chair
The Last Battle
Letters of C.S. Lewis
C.S. Lewis; A Companion and Guide

Published by
HarperCollins, San Francisco, U.S.A:
A Grief Observed

Published by Transposition UK:
Weight of Glory

Published by Macmillan, USA:
Weight of Glory

Published by Faber, U.K
A Grief Observed

Published by Harcourt Brace, U.S.A
Letters of C.S. Lewis
Surprised by Joy

Thinking Further Topics

1

C.S. Lewis loved to write stories when he was a little boy. He let his imagination take him to different worlds and amazing places. C S Lewis is a typical example of someone who was given a gift by God and who went on in later life to use this gift for the glory of God.

Do you have what you consider to be a gift? Are you gifted at music or art or sport? Think about how you can use your gift to glorify God. Perhaps you are one of those people who think that you have no gifts and that you are not particularly good at anything. Think again. Everybody has been given a gift or several gifts from God. Every day we are given 24 hours in the day. Each of these hours is a gift from God that we should use to glorify him. Are you good at making friends, listening to people or are you one of these people who just gets things organised? God wants to use you to bring others to know and love him. Memorise the following verse: Ecclesiastes 9:10. Look up these verses in the Bible, each mentions a gift from God. Thank God for these gifts today. Psalm 6:9; Psalm 130:4; Genesis 1:30; Matthew 6:25-26; 2 Peter 3:13.

2

Do you ever find it difficult to love people? Are there some people that just drive you up the wall. Some people always manage to do the very thing that infuriates you. It is important to remember if you are a Christian that you should try and be like Jesus Christ in everything that you do. How did Jesus behave with other people? Did he only hang out with the good people? Did Jesus ever ignore someone because he was too busy and couldn't be bothered. Read Matthew 19:13-14. People in Jesus time didn't always take time to listen to children. Sometimes its the same today. Jesus cared about the people no one else cared about. Can you think of someone you know who needs a friend? Try and be a good friend to someone who is lonely - just like Jesus. Perhaps there are times when people you like fall out with you or maybe you go in the huff with your Mum or Dad. Getting on with family members isn't always easy. C.S. Lewis knew that. His father wasn't always there for him and actually let him down pretty badly once or twice. We should remember that God is our heavenly father. When others let us down we can trust God always (Matthew 28:20; Proverbs 18:24.)

3

Quite often when things don't go our way we sulk and feel sorry for ourselves. We get really annoyed when we fall out with friends or when people put us down. C.S. Lewis felt discouraged when friends and colleagues thought his Narnia books were nothing special. C.S. Lewis didn't get the recognition he deserved as an academic or as a writer simply because some people did not like his strong Christian faith. The next time you feel annoyed and angry about someone think about what God would have you do. Matthew 22:37-39 gives two important rules for life. Love God first. Love others just as much as you love yourself. When someone hurts you don't hurt them back but turn to God who loves you. Ask him to help you show his love. Remember how Jesus behaved. He is our example. Even when people were hurting him and putting him to death on the cross he asked God to forgive them. Luke 23:34.

4

C.S. Lewis had many different friendships throughout his life. People who read his books would start to write to him and he always replied. Do you remember when a woman called Joy Gresham began to write to C.S. Lewis? They became firm friends and they eventually got married. It's good to have friends and people we can share things with. Are you in a relationship with God? Is God your friend? God doesn't say 'If you give me this and this I will be your friend.' God's love is something we call unconditional love. That means he loved us before we loved him. God loves us even when our lives are in the biggest mess possible. However when you become friends with someone you want to help them and do things for them don't you? Look up these verses John 15:14; John 14:15; 1 John 5:3. Can you think of anything else that you can do for God? What does God want from you in your relationship together? Proverbs 15:8 tells us that God is pleased when we pray to him. Take some time now to speak with God. If he is not your friend, ask him to be your friend now.

5

When sin came into the world sorrow and sadness came too. There is a verse in the Bible that tells us that the result of sin is death. (Romans 6:23) Because we all sin we will all die. It is a sad but true fact and it is one that we can't ignore. C.S. Lewis' mother died when he was still very young. He knew the heartache of wanting his mother when she wasn't there any more. C.S. Lewis thought that God was a magician who would wave a wand and make his mother well again, but it didn't happen. Why? Did God not hear him? Did God not care? No. God does hear and he does care. Sometimes there are just no answers or explanations for why some people die. The only reason we know about for sure is that human beings have turned away from God and that is why everything is as bad as it is. We do have hope however. Read John 3:16 to find out how God has given each of us a second chance.

The Freedom Fighter
William Wilberforce

by
Derick Bingham

'No! No!' cried the little boy, 'Please no! I want to stay with my mother!'
'Be quiet!' shouted the man who roughly pulled his mother from him. She was taken to a raised platform and offered for sale, immediately. The heart-broken mother was to be separated from her little boy for the rest of her life...

This was the fate of thousands of women and children in the days before slavery was abolished. One man fought to bring freedom and relief from the terrors of the slave trade; it took him forty-five years. His name was William Wilberforce. His exciting story shows the amazing effect his faith in Christ and his love for people had on transforming a nation.

'A story deserving to be told to a new generation.'
The Prime Minister the Rt. Hon. Tony Blair, M.P.

ISBN 1-85792-371-5

A Voice In The Dark
Richard Wurmbrand

by
Catherine Mackenzie

'Where am I? What are you doing? Where are you taking me?' Richard's voice cracked under the strain. His heart was pounding so hard he could hardly breathe. Gasping for air he realized - this was the nightmare! Thoughts came so quickly he could hardly make sense of anything.

'I must keep control,' he said out loud. An evil chuckle broke out from beside him. 'You are no longer in control. We are your worst nightmare!'...

When Richard Wurmbrand is arrested, imprisoned and tortured, he finds himself in utter darkness. Yet the people who put him there discover that their prisoner has a light which can still be seen in the dark - the love of God. This incredible story of one man's faith, despite horrific persecution, is unforgettable and will be an inspiration to all who read it.

ISBN 1-85792-298-0

From Wales to Westminster
Martyn Lloyd-Jones

by his grand-son
Christopher Catherwood

'Fire! Fire! - A woman shouted frantically. However, as the villagers desperately organised fire fighting equipment the Lloyd-Jones family slept. They were blissfully ignorant that their family home and livelihood was just about to go up in smoke. Martyn, aged ten, was snug in his bed, but his life was in danger.

What happened to Martyn? Who rescued him? How did the fire affect him and his family? And why is somebody writing a book about Martyn in the first place? In this book Christopher Catherwood, Martyn's grandson, tells you about the amazing life of his grandfather, Dr. Martyn Lloyd Jones. Find out about the young boy who trained to be a doctor at just sixteen years old. Meet the young man who was destined to become the Queen's surgeon and find out why he gave it all up to work for God. Read about Martyn Lloyd-Jones. He was enthusiastic and on fire for God. You will be, too, by the end of this book!

ISBN 1-85792-349-9

The Watch-maker's Daughter
Corrie Ten Boom

by
Jean Watson

If you like stories of adventure, courage and faith - then here's one you won't forget. Corrie loved to help others, especially handicapped children. But her happy lifestyle in Holland is shattered when she is sent to a Nazi concentration camp. She suffered hardship and punishment but experienced God's love and help in unbearable situations.

Her amazing story has been told worldwide and has inspired many people. Discover about one of the most outstanding Christian women of the 20th century.

ISBN 1-85792-116-X

LOOK OUT

FOR THE

FOLLOWING

NEW

Hudson Taylor
~ An Adventure Begins ~
by Catherine Mackenzie

GEORGE MULLER
~ The children's champion ~
by Irene Howat

Look out for our

New Fiction Titles

Something to Shout About - Sheila Jacobs.
Jane gets involved in a 'Save our Church' campaign but finds out that you can worship God anytime, anywhere.

Twice Freed - Patricia St. John.
Onesimus is a slave in Philemon's household. All he has ever wanted is to live his life in freedom. He wants nothing to do with Jesus Christ or, the man, Paul, who preaches about him. One day Onesimus steals some money from his master. Find out what happens and if Onesimus realises the meaning of true freedom!

Martin's Last Chance - Heidi Schmidt.
Rebekka and Martin live in Germany. They are firm friends and hang out everywhere together. Martin has a rare heart and lung disorder and is waiting for his last chance to get a transplant. See how Martin trust's God throughout his illness. Find out how he and Rebekka cope with the school bullies and how Rebekka finds out for herself who God is and what he is all about.

 **CHRISTIAN FOCUS**

Good books with the real message of hope!

Christian Focus Publications publishes biblically-accurate books for adults and children.

If you are looking for quality bible teaching for children then we have a wide and excellent range of bible story books - from board books to teenage fiction, we have it covered.

You can also try our new Bible teaching Syllabus for 3-9 year olds and teaching materials for pre-school children.

These children's books are bright, fun and full of biblical truth, an ideal way to help children discover Jesus Christ for themselves. Our aim is to help children find out about God and get them enthusiastic about reading the Bible, now and later in their life.

Find us at our web page:
www.christianfocus.com